VALENTINE'S ENERGY VAMPIRE DETOX

David Lloyd Strauss

Valentine's Energy Vampire Detox LLC
David Strauss
PO Box 28
Boulder, Colorado 80306

All images were created with Dall-E using custom prompts.

ORDERING INFORMATION:

Special discounts are available on quantity purchases by corporations, associations, and organizations. Contact the publisher at the above address for special discounts.

Energy Vampires is a Trademark of ENERGY VAMPIRES LLC
A Giggle Yoga Project Production
Published by Giggle Yoga LLC

Energy Vampire Series
Energy Vampire Holiday Series

*I dedicate this book
to everyone who's ready
to live an authentic life...*

*... on the path
of Personal Responsibility,
Gratitude, Forgiveness,
and Self-Love.*

*In other words,
those courageous souls
who are willing to walk away
from the darkness
and into the light.*

"It's not your job to make people love you.

*It's not your job to be somebody that you're not
so that another person will love you.*

*And it's not your job to change who you are
to meet someone else's expectations of you.*

So, what is your job?

Your job is to find the truest version of yourself.

*It means that the people who truly, love you
will love you for who you are,
not who they want you to be."*

—Unknown

CONTENTS

ROSES. CHOCOLATES. BROKEN HEARTS.

Roses are red, violets are blue,
Chocolates are sweet,
and so were you.

Among petals and sweets, a story unfolds,
Of love once warm, now bitterly cold.

Roses, they wither, their beauty decays,
Chocolates melt, in the sun's harsh rays.

So too, our love, once vibrant and bright,
Faded and broke, like the day into night.

But in every end, there's a new start,
Among thorns and sweets, beats a stronger heart.

For every rose that lost its bloom,
A bud awaits, to dispel the gloom.

Chocolates, though melted, remind us of joy,
Of moments sweet, no one can destroy.

And broken hearts, though they may ache,
Are resilient and strong, make no mistake.

So, here's to the roses, chocolates, and tears,
To love that's lost, and conquering fears.

For every ending, there's something new,
A chance to love, to live, to pursue.

—David Lloyd Strauss

ENTANGLED IN THORNES

When Valentine's Day rolls around, does it leave you feeling more alone and pained than loved and cherished?

In the season of roses and chocolates, where love is celebrated with grand romantic gestures and sweet affirmations, there lies a less-spoken truth. It's a time that can amplify the pangs of loneliness for the single-hearted and the silent struggles of those entangled in toxic relationships.

For the many people who are single and longing to have love in their lives, Valentine's Day can feel like a spotlight on solitude, a magnifying glass on your solo status, intensifying feelings of loneliness. It is a reminder of unmet desires and unshared affections. It's a day when the lack of a romantic partner can feel more pronounced, leaving a void filled with questions and doubts about your self-worth and your worthiness of love.

For those entangled in the thorns of a toxic relationship, Valentine's Day can morph from a day of love into a stark reminder of what you're missing. It's like everyone else is basking in the warm glow of love while you're stuck in a cold, shadowy corner.

You feel trapped, maybe even desperate for a way out, as if you're caught in a maze with no clear exit. The holiday amplifies the imbalance in your relationship. It's a struggle, feeling the heavy weight of a love that's supposed to uplift you but instead drags you down.

"Valentine's Detox" is here to help you find the strength to break free, to choose self-respect and self-love over staying in a harmful situation. It is for those brave souls ready to break the habit of loneliness, unshackle themselves from toxic connections, and do the inner work to find love and peace within themselves.

This is not about escaping the external forces that deplete your emotional energy; it's about rediscovering and nurturing your self-love. It's about learning to enjoy your own company, value your individuality, and understand that self-love is the first step towards attracting and fostering healthy, fulfilling relationships.

As you journey through these pages, may you find solace in solitude, strength in your struggles, and the courage to release what no longer serves your heart. May this book guide you towards a profound self-love, the kind that radiates from within and attracts the love and respect you rightfully deserve. This Valentine's season, let's redefine love as an inside job, starting with the most important person in your life — you.

Welcome to your Valentine's Detox. May your path be illuminated with self-compassion, and your heart be filled with the love that begins from within.

LOOKING FOR LOVE
IN ALL THE WRONG PLACES

What brings me to writing this book?

Let me take you back to September 2008. I was in Chaco Canyon, New Mexico, exploring ancient Anasazi ruins. The financial markets had just crashed, and I chose the solitude of the desert to search for a new direction in life. And then, bam! A rock fell from the cliff above and hit me on the head. Talk about the unexpected. This little accident kicked off a nearly five-year journey for me, one that was about healing in every way imaginable — physically, mentally, and right down to my soul.

At first, I'll admit, I saw that rock as nothing but odd luck. But as time went on, I started to see it as a hidden blessing which led to me writing my first book, *Footsteps After the Fall*. Here's the thing: on the day of that hike, I was at a critical moment in my life where, deep inside, I knew my life wasn't working. There I was, at a crossroads, carrying the weight of a painful past — a runaway at 15 due to my mother's passing, wrestling with the feelings of unworthiness and not deserving of love—that came with the many disturbing experiences that followed in my shadow of being a runaway.

But this rock, believe it or not, was the miracle I didn't even know I was looking for. I thought I was searching for a sense of purpose in Chaco Canyon, but I was on a quest to find myself — to figure out who I am and where I belong in this vast world.

I had these deep-seated feelings of being insignificant and unloved, which I'd buried deep down in my heart and mind. But don't get me wrong, my life wasn't all bad. I was living it up with adventures left and right, being an extreme athlete, traveling the world, sky diving, bungee jumping, climbing to the 23,000-foot summit of Aconcagua, Argentina, telemark skiing like a pro, and getting my thrills from rock and ice climbing.

The problem: I was hunting for love in all the wrong places—through adventure, people, food, drugs, sex, shopping, or any other form of mood-altering substances or experiences that seemed fun or interesting at the time.

I indulged in almost every experience you could imagine, believing they'd lead to the happy feeling I sought. But though I had a lot of fun mixed with a lot of pain, here's a little truth bomb for you. Love, happiness, and fulfillment are an inside job. You won't find it through other people or external situations. It's something that comes from within.

I eventually figured out that the longest journey we ever take is the one from our head to our heart. Happiness, fulfillment, self-love, and self-respect come from gratitude, forgiveness, and releasing all thoughts of blame, being a victim, or critical self-judgment.

Experience gives us perspective, but ultimately, the love we seek can only be found in our hearts and minds. I've been there, done that, got the t-shirt and trophies, and the rock showed me the true path to peace—through our hearts.

So, when it came down to writing this book, it was because I realized that for much of my life, I was on the lookout for my Valentine — that one person who'd love and accept me just as I am. But what I eventually figured out was that I hadn't even learned to love and accept myself. I was out there searching for love and validation from others without first giving myself that gift.

Valentine Detox is all about realizing that if you want true love in your life, it starts with you. It's about embracing yourself completely, with all your flaws, imperfections, and those little quirks that make you uniquely you. We've only got a limited time on this planet, so before we go seeking love from others, we need to learn how to love ourselves first.

This isn't about being perfect or having everything figured out. It's about starting where you are right now and taking it from there. Valentine's Detox is about giving yourself permission to step away from all the negativity and dysfunction in your life, especially from those who bring you down, and instead, building a loving relationship with yourself.

I'm convinced that the most impactful decision you'll ever make concerns the people you choose to surround yourself with. The people in your orbit have a far-reaching influence on your physical and mental health, wealth, confidence, and essentially every aspect of your life. They can even obscure your relationship with yourself. If your self-relationship isn't healthy, you're likely to attract people and situations that reflect your own dysfunctions.

So, here I am, single at the moment and embracing every part of who I am, ready to tell you that this book is all about learning to elevate your relationship with yourself. That's been the whole journey of my life since running away at 15 and never returning home. I've been on the road of self-development since the day I moved on my own at that young age.

Even as a runaway, I completed high school and college because I wanted my mom to be proud of me. Through it all — from being a runaway to getting hit on the head by a falling rock, and many untold quirky experiences in between, I've learned the path to self-love and self-acceptance begins with the decision to release all blame, forgive, be grateful, and accept myself first.

This book isn't me rehashing other people's ideas. It's about me inspiring you through the lens of my experience to walk away from the Energy Vampires in your life, including that Inner Vampire — your negative conversation with yourself. It's about embracing new ways of living a happy and fulfilled life.

As you read on, understand that these words are your permission slip to have the courage to walk away from the darkness and discover your inner light. Learn to love yourself first, and you'll never again have to rely on others to make you feel whole. And then, with that self-love, you can pursue and attract a life partner from a place of giving and exchanging love rather than seeking love.

Now, let's dive in and begin this journey of Valentine's Detox.

Ah, toxic relationships, what a delight,
A never-ending drama, oh what a sight.

We blame and we point, it's always their fault,
But maybe, just maybe, it's time for a halt.

Let's stop with the blaming, it's getting old,
Our own choices led us into this mold.

We thought we could change them, what a scheme,
But now it's clear, it's all just a dream.

They're not the issue, it's time to be clear,
Our decisions got us stuck in here.

So let's own up, take responsibility today,
For our own happiness, let's find a way.

No more toxic rollercoaster ride,
It's time to hop off, with a sense of pride.

No more drama, no more strife,
It's time to live a toxic-free life.

We'll chuckle at our folly, oh so wise,
As we break free from toxic ties.

Toxic relationships, we bid adieu,
It's time to rediscover ourselves anew!

—David Lloyd Strauss

PART 1

LOOK IN THE MIRROR

"Standing before the mirror, truly see yourself:
whether single and longing or in a toxic bond,
recognize your worth, embrace your truths,
and know you deserve a love
that reflects the best of you."

~David Lloyd Strauss

LOOK INTO YOUR EYES

Have you ever stood in front of the mirror and really looked at yourself? I mean, not just a quick glance while brushing your teeth, but a deep, meaningful look into your own eyes, the windows to your soul?

This mirror moment is more than just a reflection; it's the metaphorical first step in acknowledging where you are in your life. Whether you're single and longing for connection or contemplating an exit from a toxic relationship, this moment of self-reflection is crucial.

It's about confronting your reality, recognizing your desires, and understanding your current emotional landscape. For those who are single, it's a time to see beyond the societal pressure of being in a relationship and appreciate the complete, vibrant individual you are. And for countless people in a toxic relationship, it's about facing the hard truths, acknowledging the pain, and realizing that you deserve so much more.

Looking in the mirror is not just about seeing your physical self; it's about peering into your soul. What do you truly want? What are your fears? What do you need to let go of? What makes you happy? Who do you want to become? This honest introspection is the foundation upon which you can build a healthier, happier love life that starts with loving and accepting yourself first.

RELATIONSHIP MAZE

Diving into the world of relationships is like flipping through the chapters of a really good book. Each part of the story is different. With Valentine's Day around the corner, and everyone talking about detoxing from the emotional junk food in their lives, it's a great time to chat about the different stages we all go through in relationships.

Love Bubble

First up, we've got the 'Love Bubble' stage. Picture this: you're in this amazing place where you and your partner *get* each other. Everything's exciting, and you're both riding this high of being super into each other. It's like you're living in a love song, where everything your partner does feels just right.

Love's There, But It's Chill

Then, we mellow out a bit in Stage Two, 'Love's There, But It's Chill.' You're still digging each other, but the crazy fireworks have simmered down to a cozy campfire. It's comfortable, kind of like your favorite old hoodie - it feels good, but sometimes you miss that sparkly, new-shirt feeling.

Comfort Zone

Stage Three, the 'Comfort Zone,' is when things start feeling a bit too routine. It's like you're with your partner because it's easy, not because it's all fireworks and butterflies. That deep, passionate connection you had at the start? It's taken a bit of a backseat to just being each other's Netflix buddy.

Eyeing the Exit

Now, Stage Four, 'Eyeing the Exit,' is where things get real. Some days are good, but then there are those days where you're wondering what it'd be like to be single again. It's like one foot's still in the relationship and the other's inching towards the door.

Single & Searching

Stage Five, 'Single and Searching,' is when you're back out there. You're not just looking for anyone, though. You're after something real this time - a connection that's deep and meaningful.

Flying Solo and Loving It

And then there's Stage Six, 'Flying Solo and Loving It.' This is where you're totally cool with being on your own. Maybe past relationships weren't great, or maybe you're just loving the freedom. You're not actively looking for love — you're more about enjoying your own vibe and doing your own thing.

Each stage has its own flavor and lessons. They're all part of figuring out what works for you in relationships. It's about more than just finding someone; it's about understanding yourself and what makes you happy.

PLANNING YOUR ESCAPE

Valentine's Day rolls around, and there you are, not feeling the love. Instead of basking in romance, you're caught up in a reality check about your relationship. It's supposed to be a day of love and joy, but for you, it's just highlighting what you've been trying to ignore: you're in a toxic relationship, and it's draining you more than it's filling you up.

Taking a hard look at your relationship on this day can feel like opening a gift you thought was something awesome, only to find it's not what you wanted at all. That initial spark of hope and happiness has dimmed, leaving you feeling more depleted than cherished. And on Valentine's Day, of all days, the contrast between the love you hoped for and what you're living can feel stark.

You've probably tried everything to patch things up, bending over backward to make it work. It's like you're constantly adjusting, hoping to smooth over the cracks, but all it does is lead you away from your true self. It's tiring, trying to keep the peace, and it takes you down a path where you're losing sight of what matters most to you.

Thinking about breaking free? That's a big move, filled with uncertainty but also the hope of something better. It's not just about leaving a bad situation; it's about moving toward a future where you can be yourself and feel genuinely happy.

As you sit with your thoughts, the truth of your situation becomes undeniable. The manipulation, the emotional neglect—it's all too real, and deep down, you know change is necessary. Recognizing the need to walk away is tough but crucial for your well-being and happiness.

Leaving involves untangling yourself from a mess of emotions and expectations. It's a journey through guilt, shame, and the fear of what's next, mixed with the hope for a healthier, more fulfilling love. It's about confronting those feelings head-on and realizing that moving on is not just possible, it's necessary.

This process is more than a breakup; it's a journey toward self-discovery and finding a love that truly supports and uplifts you. Navigating through the complex emotions of leaving a toxic relationship is challenging, but it's also an opportunity for growth and a chance to find real happiness.

Valentine's Day, with its focus on love and connection, can magnify the loneliness and dissatisfaction in a toxic relationship. Instead of celebrating, you're left questioning why your relationship can't be like the ones you see around you. This day should be a celebration of love, but for you, it's a reminder of what's missing.

Dealing with a partner who doesn't see you, who diminishes your happiness, is exhausting. You find yourself adjusting your behavior, downplaying your needs, all for the sake of maintaining a facade of a happy relationship. But beneath the surface, there's a struggle, a longing for genuine connection and mutual respect.

This Valentine's Day might just be the wake-up call you need. It's a chance to take stock of your relationship and decide whether it's worth continuing down this path or if it's time to step away and find the happiness you deserve. It's about choosing a future where love is not just a word, but a reality that fills you with joy and fulfillment.

FROM SINGLE TO SENSATIONAL

Does this sound familiar?

Being single can feel like you're stuck in a perpetual waiting room, especially when you're yearning for a relationship. It's like everyone around you is boarding their flights to Romantic Bliss, and you're still waiting for your boarding pass. But here's the thing: being single is not a sign that you're lacking. It's not a deficit in your character or an indication that you're unlovable. In fact, it's an incredible opportunity to dig deep and find out more about yourself.

If you're riding solo through life, wishing you had a partner, the on-slaught of Valentine's romantic vibes can feel like a glaring neon sign spotlighting your single status. It's supposed to be a celebration of love, yet here it is, turning into a stark reminder of your solitude. Couples are everywhere, locked in embraces, and social media is flooded with heart memes and lovey-dovey posts, making your solo journey feel all the more empty. It's a day that stirs up a storm of emotions, from lone-liness to longing, making you question your worthiness.

Amidst this sea of hand-holding couples and heart-shaped candies, spiraling into self-doubt is easy. You wonder, "Why does love seem to evade me?" or "Is something wrong with me?" The day's focus on romance unintentionally spotlights your current singlehood, turning what could be a joyous day into a session of deep introspection, maybe even sadness.

On a day like this, the absence of romance can feel like a gaping hole. The media bombards the entire planet with images of idealized love, widening the gap between your reality and these fairy-tale romances.

But here's where "Valentine's Detox" flips the script. It challenges you to change the narrative from what's missing to what's possible during this time. Instead of seeing singleness as a shortfall, view it as a golden opportunity for personal growth and exploration—a sliver in time to dive deep into understanding yourself, your desires, and your dreams.

Being single is a priceless moment in time to focus on yourself. It's an uninterrupted chance to explore your passions, free from the con-straints of a relationship. Use this time to pursue growth in areas that interest you and build a fulfilling life on your own terms.

This phase of singleness isn't about what you don't have. It's about the richness you can discover within. It's an invitation to turn inward, adopt a loving relationship with yourself, and create a whole and satisfy-ing life, with or without a partner. "Valentine's Detox" transforms your perspective, turning this period into an empowering space brimming with your interests, passions, and aspirations. It's a priceless chance to grow, evolve, and become the most vibrant version of yourself.

So, let's talk about the search for your "other half." It's a common theme in love stories and an underlying hope for so many people—that there's someone out there who can complete you. But isn't this thought a bit misleading? By seeking your other half, you are subtly saying that you are only half a person to begin with. But hold on — is finding your "other half" really love?

True love, is it about discovering someone who fills in your gaps, or is it about bringing a whole, fulfilled self to the table? Do you really want to bring an incomplete version of yourself into a relationship? Maybe, just maybe, what we've been calling love is often just dependency dressed up in the robes of romance.

When you're on the hunt for someone to make you feel loved and whole, you're essentially handing over the keys to your happiness to someone else. It's placing your fulfillment and self-worth in another's hands. The truth is, no one should hold that kind of power over your happiness; it's something you develop within.

Real love is about finding someone who complements the whole, complete person you already are. It's not about dependency; it's about partnership—someone to learn and grow with, to create new memories and enjoy the nuances of life. Looking for a relationship to solve your loneliness or fill a void isn't love; it's seeking validation.

The real magic is not in what you can get from a relationship but in who you become to attract the right person. It's about being the best version of yourself, for yourself. When you nurture self-love and self-respect, you become a magnet for someone who values those same qualities. Remember, you attract what you are, not what you desire. So, if you're after a loving, fulfilling relationship, first create those qualities within yourself—the loving version of yourself who is living a fulfilled life— and you will attract a person with those qualities.

Constantly seeking someone to complete you is chasing a mirage. True completeness comes from being at peace with yourself, knowing your strengths and weaknesses, doing what you love, and being the authentic, loving version of yourself. Once you reach this state of self-acceptance, you stop looking for someone to fill a void; instead, you seek someone with whom to share your already satisfying life.

The journey to finding true love is as much about self-discovery and personal growth as it is about finding the right partner. Become the person who embodies the qualities you seek in a partner, and you're more likely to attract that genuinely fun, adventurous, enriching relationship you desire.

In the midst of Valentine's Day, if you're single, it's tempting to feel overshadowed by the festivities around you. But let's change that perspective: being single isn't a setback; it's a chance for personal empowerment. "From Single to Sensational" isn't just a catchy phrase; it's a mindset about owning and celebrating yourself as you are right now, while welcoming new experiences to expand your experience of life. It's about realizing that this phase is an invaluable opportunity for self-improvement and growth.

Instead of seeing singleness as a gap to be filled, view it as a space for personal expansion. It's the ideal time to explore your interests, set goals, and work on aspects of yourself that have been on the back burner. Think of it as laying a solid foundation for any future relationship.

Being single offers the unique advantage of focusing solely on your needs and aspirations. Use this time to build your self-esteem, develop your skills, improve your health, or even travel and explore new hobbies. This self-growth makes you more attractive to the right person when they come along.

The notion that you need someone else to complete you is a myth. True fulfillment comes from within. It's about knowing your worth, understanding your values, and being comfortable in your own skin. When you expand these aspects of your life, you naturally attract people who appreciate the confident, well-rounded person you are.

Remember, attracting the right person isn't about seeking someone who fills a gap in your life. It's about finding someone who appreciates the complete person you already are. So, use this single time to focus on becoming the best version of yourself. It's not just about preparing for a future relationship but about being sensational on your own terms. Embrace this journey from single to sensational, where your growth and self-discovery shape a life that's as fulfilling alone as it would be with a partner.

PART 2

EMBRACE THE INNER JOURNEY

In the dance of light and shadow,
where dreams are chased and fears battled,
A journey unfolds, a path untold, where the heart grows bold
and stories are retold. Through the valleys of doubt
and the peaks of despair, comes a whisper on the wind,
a call to those who dare.

Embrace the journey, for it's yours to own, Through the thorns of
past, where seeds of hope are sown. Let the dance of life, with its
twists and turns, Ignite the fire within, as the soul yearns.

For beyond the darkness, beyond the night, lies a dawn of strength,
bathed in light. Where energy vampires lurk and shadows play, there
lies a power, to push them away.

With every step, with every breath, Challenge the inner vampire,
defy the specter of death. For in the heart's deepest chambers, pure
and true, Lies the courage to begin, to start anew.

Through toxic ties that bind and weave, Comes the strength to fight,
to believe. In the beauty of letting go, in the grace of moving on, Lies
the wisdom of the ages, the light of the dawn.

So, embrace the journey, with all its pain and glory, for every fall,
every rise, tells your story. From the ashes of the old, let the new life
emerge, Ride the waves of change,
let your true self surge.

Embrace the journey, for it's beautifully complex,
A tapestry of moments, a mosaic of reflex.
With gratitude as your compass, forgiveness as your guide,
Step into the journey, with your heart open wide.

—David Lloyd Strauss

THREE ENEMIES OF SELF-LOVE

Whether you're single during the Valentine's holiday or planning your escape from a toxic relationship, the real work lies within. It comes down to realizing that the most important relationship you will ever have is the one with yourself. Your self-talk, habits, beliefs, and the people you associate with are all a part of your relationship with yourself.

Many people grapple with the three enemies of self-love: feelings of unworthiness, not being good enough, or believing they don't deserve love. These feelings are more common than you might think and play a pivotal role in how we perceive ourselves and our relationships with others. The first step in our journey is acknowledging these deep-seated emotions and understanding their impact on our lives.

Unworthiness

Valentine's Detox is a time for more than just reevaluating our romantic connections; it's also about facing up to those nagging feelings of unworthiness that often keep us stuck in unhappy relationships. With all the lovey-dovey stuff in the air during Valentine's Day, if you're wrestling with these feelings, it can hit harder. It's like staring into a mirror that doesn't just show your single status or relationship woes, but also zooms in on that deep-seated belief that you are unworthy of the love and connection you desire.

Feeling unworthy is like having an emotional filter that dims your strengths and blows up your flaws. It's hanging out in a crowd but feeling totally alone, stuck with the thought that you don't fit in or aren't as entitled to happiness and love as everyone else. It's that sneaky voice that shadows your achievements, whispering, "You're a phony, and pretty soon, everyone's going to figure it out."

This mindset can creep into every corner of your life. Maybe in your love life, it shows up as settling for less because deep down, you think that's all you deserve. Or maybe it's like hitting the self-destruct button on relationships or other situations that actually make you happy, because part of you believes happiness isn't meant for you. It could mean staying silent when your inner voice is screaming, keeping you stuck in a cycle of what-ifs and if-only's.

Often, these feelings stem from way back — maybe a childhood where you didn't hear enough praise or where love felt like something you had to earn. Those external voices from way back when becoming the voice of your Inner Energy Vampire—the self-talk that strangles your belief in yourself. The external voices can become your own, replaying the same old criticisms and conditions in your head, but now, they are your identity of not being worthy.

But there's light at the end of the tunnel, and it's not the headlight of a train; it is the light of hope and possibilities. These feelings of unworthiness? They're not set in stone. They're more like a story we've been telling ourselves, and stories can be rewritten. It starts with questioning those negative self-beliefs. It's about being kind to yourself and realizing that it's okay to be imperfect and still be worthy of all the good life has to offer. Celebrate the small wins, learn from the slip-ups, and surround yourself with people who lift you up and remind you of your worth, especially when you forget.

Getting past these feelings of unworthiness is a journey. It's not a quick fix; it's a road that takes patience and effort. It's about gradually building up a more positive, realistic self-image that sees and accepts your worth and embraces your humanity, flaws and all. Along the way, you start to feel lighter, more hopeful, and ready to embrace life's opportunities. You begin to recognize that you deserve love, respect, and happiness, not because you've become someone different, but because you've realized you were always enough.

Consider these questions:

- When do you usually feel least worthy? What are the thoughts or beliefs about yourself that feed into these feelings?

- How have your past experiences colored your view of your worth, and what steps can you take to challenge and change these old narratives?

Not Good Enough

If there's one belief that collapses relationships, has us choosing the wrong partners, or keeps us single, it's that nagging sense of "Not Good Enough." How we see ourselves, our self-image, is our point of attraction. It sets the tone for everything. It's like wearing glasses that color how we view the world and who we let into our lives. If we're walking around looking through the lenses of "not good enough," it's like we're sending out an invitation to attract relationships that mirror that belief.

If you have ever felt like you're not good enough to be loved, you're not alone. Countless people struggle with this persistent shadow of doubt, haunted by a nagging sense of being unworthy of love.

You know that nagging feeling, right? The one that quietly whispers, "I'm just not good enough for love." It's like an internal thief, stealing away our hopes and aspirations for love. This voice criticizes everything. "I'm too heavy," "I'm too thin," "My hair's a mess," "I'm too short," "I'm not attractive enough," I'm not smart enough." It's a struggle so many people face, this sense of unworthiness in love. It's like carrying an invisible backpack heavy with doubts and insecurities.

This whole "not good enough" thing usually boils down to a super-critical inner voice—the voice of your internal energy vampire sucking the happiness from your soul. It's like having a personal critic on loop in your mind, constantly highlighting your mistakes and flaws—as if you're looking at yourself through a funhouse mirror that only shows the worst parts.

Living with this self-sabotage, energy vampire mindset is like being locked in a room of your own making, where the walls are painted with all the negative stuff you think about yourself, constantly reminding you of your flaws. It's a self-perpetuating cycle. When you think you don't deserve love, you might push people away or choose partners who confirm this belief by treating you poorly.

But here's the kicker — you can break out of this cycle. It starts with being a bit kinder to yourself by releasing the self-judgment. Everyone's got flaws, everyone messes up — that's part of being human. Learning to forgive yourself and understanding that you deserve love and intimacy is the first step.

Self-kindness begins with first recognizing when those "not good enough" buttons get pushed. Maybe it's social settings where you don't quite fit in. It's like everyone else has a handbook on how to be cool and confident, and you're just winging it. This can make you feel like you're on the outside looking in, feeding into the idea that you're somehow less deserving of love and connection. These feelings can trap you in a loop of staying single because you don't think anyone would want you—or keep you stuck in a toxic relationship because you don't believe you deserve better.

Breaking this loop begins with a shift in your internal dialogue. Celebrate your wins and focus on your strengths. Everyone has something special, something unique and attractive — it's time you recognize those gems within yourself. Surrounding yourself with positive people makes a huge difference. Being with people who see your worth and remind you of it can help rewrite those internal stories you tell yourself.

Remember, the journey from feeling like you're not enough to knowing you're worthy of love is like a road trip. There are ups and downs, but it's filled with opportunities for growth and self-discovery. Start to view yourself through a kinder lens, and you open the door to healthier relationships — with others and, most importantly, with yourself.

Consider these questions:

* What's one thing I did recently that I'm proud of?
* How can I remind myself daily that I'm worthy just as I am?

Overcoming these feelings of *not good enough* isn't just about improving your self-image; it's about enhancing your whole experience of life. It's about stepping into a world where you feel deserving of all the good life has to offer — all the love, joy, and fulfillment, and everything in between.

Not Deserving of Love

Have you ever felt like love is a private club, and you don't have the secret handshake to get in and enjoy the fun? Like no matter what you do, you're on the outside looking in, thinking love is meant for everyone else but you? This feeling, this nagging sense of not deserving love, is more common than you'd think. It's like carrying around an invisible sign that says, "Love? Not for me, thanks."

Let's get real about this. Feeling undeserving of love is like living with a constant, low-grade fever — it doesn't knock you out, but it saps your energy and colors your view of the world. It can wiggle into your life in sneaky ways. Maybe you downplay compliments, shrug off affection, or laugh off the idea of someone falling for you. Or perhaps you're the first to joke about being "forever alone." Sure, it's a protective shield, but it's also a lonely fortress.

This feeling doesn't just pop up out of nowhere. It's often rooted in deeper memories — past hurts, rejections, maybe growing up in an environment where love felt conditional or just plain scarce. These experiences can stick to you like shadows, whispering that you're not lovable enough.

Here's the twist — feeling undeserving of love can make you a magnet for relationships that reinforce this belief. Have you ever found yourself in a situation where you're bending over backward for someone who gives you the bare minimum? Or sticking around in a relationship that feels more draining than fulfilling? It's like your heart is working on a self-fulfilling prophecy: "I don't deserve better, so I won't look for better."

But guess what? You can flip the script. Start by taking a good, hard look at those beliefs. Ask yourself where they're coming from. Are they based on old stories you've been telling yourself? Harmful words spoken to you by others? Recognizing these beliefs as just thoughts, not truths, is a game-changer.

Next up, it's time for some serious self-love. And no, it's not just bubble baths and face masks (though those are nice!). It's about treating yourself with the same kindness and compassion you'd offer a good friend. Celebrate your wins, however small. Forgive yourself for not being perfect. Remember, you're a work in progress, and that's okay.

Surround yourself with positive people. The kind who lifts you up, who see the awesome person you are, and aren't shy about telling you. Their voices can help drown out that critical inner voice that's been hogging the mic for too long.

Most importantly, start rewriting your love story. Imagine what it would be like to truly believe you deserve love. How would you act? What choices would you make? How would you treat yourself and others? Start living that story, bit by bit, day by day.

Remember, feeling like you don't deserve love is just a chapter in your life, not the whole book. You have the power to write the next chapters, and they can be filled with love, respect, and happiness. You deserve it, even if you're still learning to believe it.

Let's pause and reflect on these three enemies of self-love: Unworthiness, Not Good Enough, and Not Deserving Love—the common threads that often weave silently through our lives.

The feeling of unworthiness. This sneaky intruder, along with its close cousins 'not good enough' and 'undeserving of love', can really throw a wrench in our quest for healthy, fulfilling relationships. So, how do we break free from this invisible cage?

Picture this: You're standing in front of a mirror, but instead of your reflection, it shows every critical word, every doubt, and every instance you've been told or felt you weren't enough. This mirror doesn't reflect reality; it reflects the distorted perceptions and beliefs that have been ingrained in us over time.

Many of us carry the weight of feeling unworthy, often without even realizing it. It's like walking around with invisible shackles, limiting our steps towards happiness and fulfillment. Whether it's a whisper from the past or a recent sting of rejection, these feelings can take a front seat in our minds, steering us towards relationships that don't serve us well or keeping us trapped in loneliness.

The feeling of 'not being good enough' often comes from a place of deep vulnerability. It's that voice that tells us we're not smart enough, attractive enough, successful enough — just never quite enough for love or happiness. This mindset can lead us to settle for less, to shrink our dreams and desires, or worse, to push away the very love we crave.

Being 'undeserving of love' is another facet of this inner struggle. It convinces us that there's something fundamentally unlovable about us. Maybe it's an error we made, a path we chose, or just an inherent flaw we believe we have. This feeling is a significant roadblock in our quest for love, as it persuades us that no matter what we do, we'll never be worthy of true affection and belonging.

The truth is, these feelings don't have to dictate our lives. They're not unchangeable facts, but beliefs that we have the power to reshape.

The first step is to recognize and confront these feelings. Acknowledge them not as truths, but as the echoes of past experiences and external judgments. This recognition is powerful—it's the first steam to ridding your mind of these emotional enemies.

Next, practice self-compassion and challenge the inner critic. Replace this story with reminders of your strengths, achievements, and qualities. You are a unique blend of talents, thoughts, and experiences — and that in itself is enough.

Lastly, understand that you are inherently deserving of love. It's not something you earn; it's something you're born with. You are worthy of love and happiness just by being you.

Thoughts

As we prepare to learn more about the role Energy Vampires and Your Inner Vampire play in your life, here are three questions to consider:

- What specific experiences or voices from your past add to your feelings of unworthiness, and how can you start to release their hold?
- When you look at your achievements and strengths, what are the qualities you value most in yourself, and how can they counteract the feeling of not being good enough?
- How can you actively practice self-compassion every day to reinforce your belief that you deserve love and happiness?

Remember, this journey of self-discovery and self-love is not just about liberating yourself from toxicity, it's about creating a life where you are the hero of your story, not the side character shadowed by unworthiness. It's about stepping into the light of self-acceptance and embracing the love that you rightly deserve.

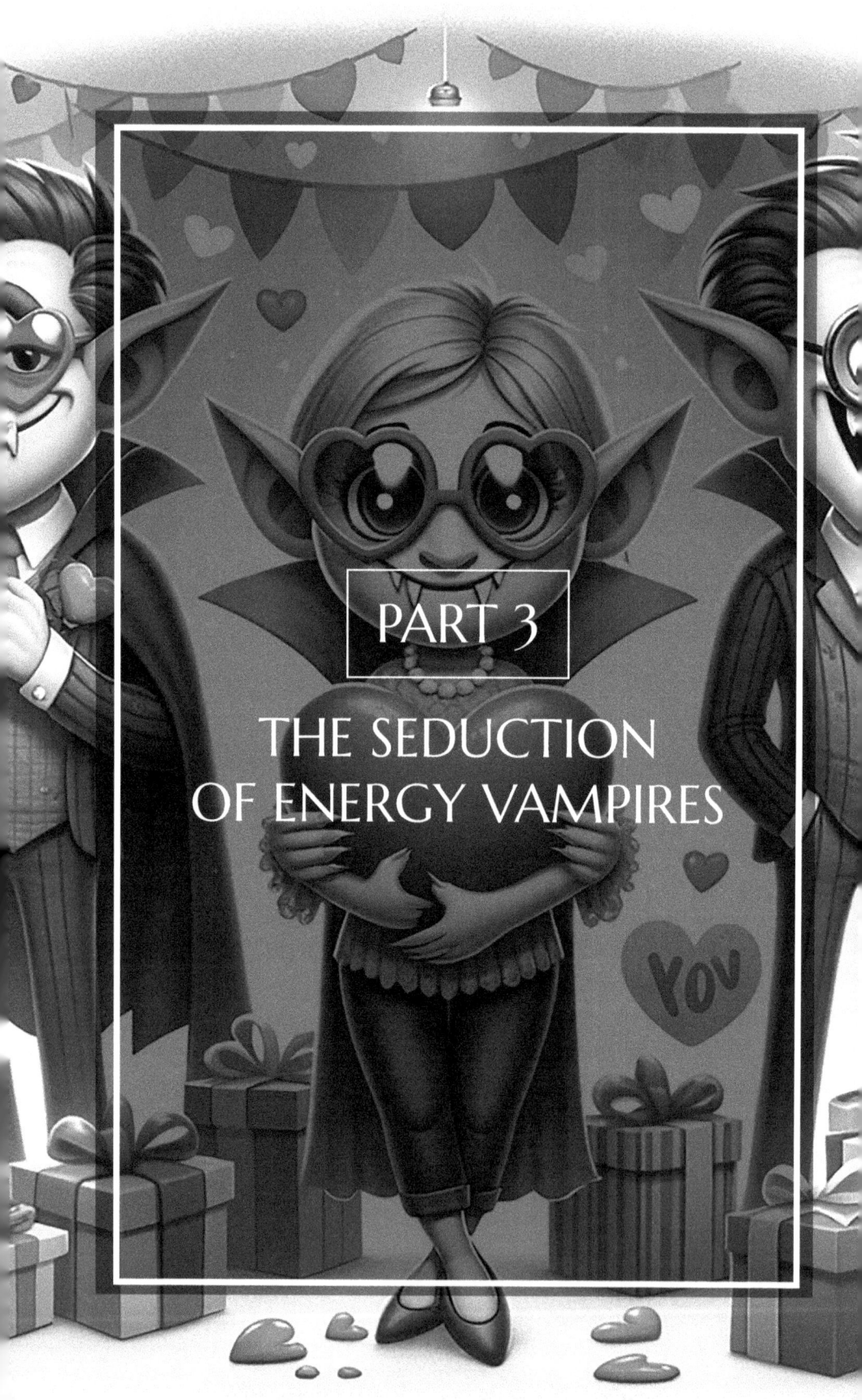

PART 3

THE SEDUCTION
OF ENERGY VAMPIRES

In a world spun of sunlight and shade, Where Energy Vampires prowl and parade, beware, dear heart, their charming charade, for the are crafty creatures, expertly made.

They'll whisper sweet nothings, promise the moon, but their intentions make angels swoon, with a grin and a wink, they'll dance you 'round, till your feet barely touch the ground.

But hold your laughter, keep your grace, don't let them pull you into their embrace. For their touch is ice, their words spun from frost, in their game of take, it's you who'll be lost.

Wear a smile like armor, light as a feather, Navigate their storms, no matter the weather. For you are the sun, radiant and bright, against your glow, they'll vanish from sight.

So, here's to you, the merry and wise, who see through the vampires' clever disguise. Dance your own dance, sing your own song, In the light of your truth, you'll always belong.

With a wink and a nod, let's raise our cup, To a life well-lived and spirits up. For in the end, it's laughter and love that wins, Against the shadows, and all their sins.

A DATE WITH ENERGY VAMPIRES

So, we've been deep-diving into our feelings of unworthiness, not good enough, and not deserving love. It's like we've been on a personal treasure hunt, getting real with what's in our hearts. But now, there's another chapter in our journey of self-love discovery. We're about to unmask the Energy Vampires. And no, we're not talking about spooky characters from a movie.

Energy Vampires are those real-life people who nefariously drain your mental, emotional, and spiritual energy, leaving you more like a deflated balloon than a shooting star. As we step into this new area, it's not about pointing blame or judging. It's about learning to recognize and deflect the negative people in our lives so we can accept responsibility for our overall health, happiness, and well-being. Understanding how to handle these emotional drainers is key to keeping all that self-love and self-worth we've been nurturing.

There is also the Inner Vampire. It's not as spooky as it sounds. It's actually a metaphor for all that negative self-chatter and those deep insecurities that sometimes pull us into not-so-great relationships. Knowing how this Inner Vampire works is crucial for changing the patterns that attract unhealthy relationships.

Then there's the whole conversation we have with ourselves. Our values, standards, and expectations shape how we talk to ourselves, affecting the kind of relationships we pull into our orbit. By diving into the questions we ask ourselves, we can start to shift our mindset and open the door to more fulfilling interactions.

Valentine's Day is supposed to be all about love, chocolates, and maybe some fancy dinner. But let's be real — sometimes, it feels more like opening Pandora's box in our relationships, especially when dealing with those pesky Energy Vampires. You know, the ones who can drain the life out of what should be a pretty awesome day. It's time to take a deep dive into identifying these sneaky energy drainers and figuring out how to kick them out of our love lives.

Picture this: You're psyched for a day filled with love, but instead, you're dealing with a partner who's all about themselves. Maybe they're downplaying your efforts to make the day special, or worse, they're turning the whole thing into some emotional rollercoaster. Suddenly, Valentine's Day is less about romance and more about survival, trying to dodge the emotional bullets they keep firing your way.

Energy Vampires aren't just one type — they come in all shapes and sizes. There's the classic Taker, always about what they need, leaving you feeling like an emotional ATM. Or the Drama Queen, who loves to stir the pot just when things should be chill. And let's not forget the Blamers, the masters of making everything your fault, or the super insecure ones, who need constant reassurance that yes, they're still the apple of your eye.

On Valentine's Day, these Energy Vampires can really ramp up their game. It's like they know you're hoping for some fairytale romance, and they use that to push your buttons even more. Whether it's guilt-tripping you for more attention or just ignoring all the effort you've put in, they know how to turn a day of love into a test of your patience. Dealing with this can take a toll. You might end up feeling anxious, or even start doubting yourself — classic signs you're dealing with a pro Energy Vampire. It's more than just a bummer; it can make you question your entire relationship and leave you feeling pretty low.

Energy Vampires have many faces, flavors, and personalities. Not all of them are inherently bad people. Some are just like you and I; they had a rough patch in their lives, and being hurtful or controlling is their coping mechanism for avoiding pain. Even so, whatever the reason, let's break down the different types of Energy Vampires, see how they can mess with what should be a pretty sweet day, and most importantly, figure out how to show them the door. It's about taking back your Valentine's Day (and your life) and ensuring your love life is more about—love.

By understanding these Energy Vampires, we can turn Valentine's Day back into what it should be: a day to celebrate love, starting with loving ourselves and spreading that vibe to all our relationships. So, let's dive in and get our love life detox started, shall we?

IS YOUR PARTNER AN ENERGY VAMPIRE?

Have you ever wondered if your partner might be an Energy Vampire? You know, the kind who always finds a way to control, manipulate, or belittle you, making you feel unworthy or unloved.

And then there's the Energy Vampire wo seems always to need more from you - more attention, more reassurance, more everything. No matter how much you give, it feels like it's never enough. It's like pouring all your love and effort into a bottomless pit; your energy vanishes without making any impact. That's classic Energy Vampire behavior right there.

These partners are masters at sucking the joy out of situations. They seem to thrive on creating drama, turning even the smallest issues into full-blown crises. It's their way of hogging the spotlight, ensuring that your energy is constantly directed towards them. And before you know it, you're caught up in their whirlwind of chaos, leaving little room for your own needs and feelings.

The tricky part? These types can be incredibly charming, especially in the beginning. They reel you in with their sweet, caring nature, making you feel special and loved. But as time goes on, their true colors start to show. They begin to drain your emotional energy, one crisis, one demand, one critical comment at a time. Some of these Energy Vampires can be pretty controlling too. They're like emotional manipulators, taking advantage of your kindness or playing on your insecurities.

If they sense you have feelings of being unworthy of love, not good enough, or not deserving of love, they might use this to their advantage. They'll subtly manipulate and control you, often in ways so subtle you don't even realize it's happening. It's a gradual process; before you know it, you're too deep to step back easily.

Being in a relationship with an Energy Vampire can be exhausting. You find yourself constantly trying to meet their needs and expectations, but it never seems to be enough. It's like being on an emotional treadmill — you're running all the time but getting nowhere. This can leave you feeling drained, both emotionally and physically, and can even start to affect your self-esteem and sense of self-worth.

Remember, love is supposed to be about mutual support and growth, not about one person constantly taking while the other gives. A healthy relationship should make you feel uplifted and energized, not drained and depleted. If you find yourself in a relationship with an Energy Vampire, it might be time to reevaluate and consider what you really want and deserve in a partnership.

Being with an Energy Vampire can really take a toll on you. But here's the silver lining: Recognizing the signs of Energy Vampires is the first step towards rebuilding your heart and your deservingness of true love. Understanding that you're in the clutches of an Energy Vampire gives you permission to take action. It's about setting boundaries, reclaiming your energy, and remembering that a healthy relationship should enhance your life, not diminish it.

So, if you're asking yourself, "Is my partner an Energy Vampire?" it might be time to look closely at your relationship. Remember, love should leave you feeling revitalized, not drained. It's about mutual support, respect, and growth, not about one person constantly taking while the other gives.

Now let's take a closer look at the Energy Vampires that overshadow our hearts.

THE ENERGY VAMPIRES

Imagine opening your emotional closet, the place where you hide and bury your past pain for no one to see and finding it's not just skeletons lurking there but Energy Vampires. These aren't your spooky movie types; no, these are real people in your life who, knowingly or not, can suck your emotional energy dry. Since we are on a quest to detox from toxic relationships, let's shine a light on these sneaky emotional Dracula's.

Visualize a world filled with different kinds of Energy Vampires. They're like characters in a not-so-fun emotional drama, each with their unique way of draining your spirit. They pop up everywhere — at work, in your family, and even in your love life. They're the ones who leave you feeling like an over-squeezed lemon after every interaction.

The challenge with Energy Vampires is they are disconnected from their own sources of positivity. Whether it is a fracture in their personality from trauma or a genetic break that affects their ability to feel empathy, Energy Vampires are very much like moths. Just as moths are attracted to an outside light at night, they are drawn to other people's energy because they cannot connect with their own source of light. So, they latch onto others like emotional parasites on the prowl.

Here's a quick peek at a few of the most common Energy Vampires and then we'll go into greater detail.

The Takers: Picture someone with a 'What's in it for me?' attitude. They're like emotional black holes, always needing, taking, but rarely giving back. It's like being with someone who has an unquenchable thirst for your attention and energy.

The Blamers: Oh, these people, they're like walking, talking complaint boxes. Nothing is ever their fault. It's always someone else's — and often, that someone is you. Dealing with them is like playing an endless game of 'It's not me, it's you.'

The Crabs: Ever met someone who can't stand to see you happy? That's them. They're so insecure they try to drag you down to their level. Masters of the underhanded compliment, they leave you feeling deflated and doubting yourself.

The Wannabes: Always green with envy, the Wannabes are trapped in a cycle of comparing themselves (and you) to everyone else. They're like emotional vacuums, sucking the joy out of your achievements and successes.

The Drama Queens: Life for them is a never-ending telenovela. There's always a crisis, and somehow, you're the co-star in their drama. They're experts in turning a molehill into a mountain and expect you to be their constant savior.

Identifying these characters in your life is a game-changer, especially when you're trying to detox from those not-so-great relationships. It's all about understanding these draining dynamics and learning to protect your precious emotional energy.

Let's dive in and uncover their many faces and facades, and ways to navigate these tricky waters and steer towards healthier, more fulfilling relationships. It's about turning the page to a chapter where you're not just surviving these emotional traps but thriving beyond them. Let's embark on this eye-opening journey together, shall we?

Now, instead of scratching the surface, let's shine a magnifying glass on each of these emotional parasites.

TAKERS: MASTERS OF NARCISSISM

Let's dive into the world of 'Takers.' These people are like peacocks, all showy and needing to be the star. They love the spotlight, thrive on admiration, and struggle with the whole empathy thing.

In the dating world, narcissists come across as the dream package — all charm and fairy-tale romance. But as the fairy dust settles, you might see the not-so-charming side. It's like buying a shiny apple and finding it's rotten inside. They can twist your words and make you doubt yourself — it's like being in an emotional hall of mirrors.

Breaking free from those toxic relationships can really be an eye-opener, especially when you're dealing with someone who's a pro at manipulating. These Takers, also known as narcissists, have a way of making everything about them, and it's a pretty clever game they play.

Picture this: You're all set to share something about your day, and suddenly, this person is turning the entire conversation around to focus on themselves. It's like they're the sun, and everyone else orbits around them. They've got this charm, but it has an agenda. It's all about them, 24/7.

Narcissists are the ultimate takers in a World of Givers. They've got this magnetic pull towards people who are natural givers, kind to the core, and big-hearted lovers who avoid conflict at all costs. It's like they have a radar for detecting people who love deeply, care immensely, and say 'yes' a bit too easily.

Why Givers Attract Narcissists

Narcissists are on a constant hunt for attention and admiration. Now, who better to provide this than the givers? These generous souls, often putting others first, become an ideal source of the endless affirmation narcissists crave. Givers radiate warmth and care, and narcissists bask in this glow, often taking more than their share.

Conflict Avoidance: A Narcissist's Playground

People who shy away from confrontation are like gold for a narcissist. Why? Because narcissists love a smooth ride, a path with no resistance. Someone who avoids conflict is less likely to call them out or challenge them, letting the narcissist have their way. It's like having a remote control for the relationship; the narcissist presses the buttons, and the conflict-avoider follows suit, often to keep the peace.

Kindness — A Double-Edged Sword

There's something about a kind-hearted person that draws a narcissist in. Kind people often jump in to help, to understand, and to support. Narcissists can twist this kindness to their advantage, often playing the victim or the misunderstood hero. It's a manipulation tactic, turning kindness into a tool for their own gain.

Lovers and Romantics: Easy Targets

Lovers, those who love with all they've got, can sometimes get caught in the narcissist's web. Narcissists can be charming, making grand gestures of love, creating this whirlwind romance that feels too good to be true. And, well, often it is. It's a game of smoke and mirrors, where the narcissist plays the role of a perfect partner, only to drop the act once they've got their hooks in deep enough.

Understanding the Taker's Game

At the heart of it, narcissists are takers. They're in it for what they can get — attention, control, admiration. They see relationships more like transactions — what can this person do for me? The sad part is, their need for the spotlight often overshadows any real capacity for genuine, selfless love. Here's a quick rundown:

The Conversational Hoarder: Have you ever found yourself in a conversation where you can't get a word in? Yup, that's a Taker for you. They dominate the conversation, and if you manage to say something, they'll somehow spin it back to them. It's downright exhausting and leaves you feeling like you're just an extra in your own life's movie.

The Chronic One-Upper: These people love the spotlight. Share a small win, and they'll trump it with something bigger. It's their way of staying on top, even if it means minimizing your achievements. It's not just annoying; it can be pretty disheartening.

The Validation Seeker: They might look like they're listening, but it's a ruse. They're on a constant hunt for compliments and affirmations. It's all about feeding their ego, with little to no emotional support coming your way.

The Emotional Manipulator: Takers are really good at this game. They'll twist situations, making you feel guilty for not meeting their every demand. And if things don't go their way, guess who gets the blame? Yep, you guessed it.

The Boundary Pusher: Personal space? That's a foreign concept to them. They'll demand your time and energy without any sense of reciprocation. And if you dare set boundaries, they'll make you feel like the villain for not being at their beck and call.

Dealing with narcissists can feel like you're in a one-sided relationship where you're the only one making an effort. It's emotionally draining and can leave you feeling pretty hollow. Recognizing these traits is liberating, especially when you're in the process of detoxing from an unhealthy relationship.

These partners are the epitome of selfishness in relationships. They're only emotionally available when it benefits them, making everything revolve around their needs and desires. Conversations with Takers are often one-sided, where you're reduced to being just a listener to their endless monologues. They're experts in subtly twisting situations to their advantage, often at your emotional expense.

Dealing with a Taker in a relationship is like trying to fill a bottomless cup — exhausting and ultimately futile. But don't worry. Once you know what to look out for, you're halfway to solving the problem. So, let's break it down with a dash of chill and a sprinkle of real talk.

Spotting a Taker: Picture this: You're pouring your heart out, and all you get in return is a nod before the conversation swivels back to them. Classic Taker move. They're smooth operators, often cloaked in charm, making it tricky to spot their selfish streak initially. But if you constantly feel like a background singer in your own life's song, chances are you're dealing with a Taker. They're like emotional magicians — skilled at diverting attention and guilt-tripping you into feeling responsible for their happiness. It's a sneaky game of emotional tug-of-war.

Detoxing from a Taker

Alright, here's your game plan. You're dealing with a taker — someone who's mastered the art of taking without giving much back. Here's how you break free.

Step 1: Spot the Signs. Grab a notepad or your phone. Jot down the moments you felt more like a resource than a partner. This isn't about making them the villain; it's about seeing the situation clearly. Think of it as mapping the terrain before planning your route.

Step 2: Imagine Your Ideal Day. What does a day look like without walking on eggshells or constantly giving without receiving? Sketch this out. It's your destination post-detox.

Step 3: Build Your Exit Plan. Start small. Maybe it's setting a boundary today and sticking to it. Perhaps it's reaching out to a friend or family member you've been distant from. Every step, no matter how small, is part of your journey out.

Step 4: Gather Your Squad. You know those friends who always say, "If you ever need anything…"? Time to take them up on it. Share your plan, or just let them know you're going through a tough time. You're not alone in this.

Step 5: Self-Care Like a Boss. This is crucial. Your energy and self-esteem have taken hits. What fills you up? Yoga? Reading? Long walks? Do more of that. It's like charging your batteries for the journey ahead.

Step 6: D-Day (Detox Day). When you're ready, make your move. This could mean a conversation, a letter, or taking physical steps away from the relationship. It's not just about leaving; it's about moving towards something better.

Step 7: Reflect and Rebuild. Once you're out, take time to reflect. What did you learn? How have you grown? Then, start building that ideal day you imagined. Piece by piece, day by day.

Remember, planning your escape from a taker is about recognizing you deserve more. It's about understanding that for all the energy and love you put out, you should be receiving just as much in return. And when that's not happening, it's okay to say, "This isn't for me," and walk towards what is.

So, here's to recognizing the dysfunction, crafting a plan, and stepping into a life where your needs, dreams, and well-being are front and center. Here's to you and your new beginning. Cheers!

DRAMA QUEEN WEBS

Valentine's Detox is the perfect time to address the Drama Queens in romantic relationships. These are the partners who seem to live for conflict and emotional upheaval, making every little issue a major drama. Here's a closer look at the types you might encounter:

Drama Queens turn life into a soap opera with a daily twist. When you're on a mission to detox from toxic relationships, they're like the plot twist you didn't sign up for. So, let's break it down.

The Allure of the Drama Queen

Drama Queens: they're magnetic, aren't they? With their lives like a never-ending soap opera, full of twists and turns, they draw us in. It's the intensity of their emotions, the highs and lows, that makes everything seem so much more exciting. But here's the catch - while it's entertaining to watch, being part of the drama is a whole different story.

Caught in the Web

Getting involved with a Drama Queen can feel like being caught in a web. Initially, it's thrilling. You feel needed and important as you're pulled into their world of constant crisis. But soon, you realize it's not just their world you're living in; it's their drama. And this drama, it's exhausting. It drains your energy, leaving little room for your own needs and feelings.

The Emotional Rollercoaster

Being close to a Drama Queen means you're on an emotional rollercoaster that never stops. One day, you're the hero, the only one who understands and can help. The next, you're the villain, accused of not caring enough or being there. This constant upheaval of emotions can be bewildering, leaving you unsure of where you stand.

The Quest for Stability

After a while, you start craving stability. You long for a relationship that's based on mutual respect and understanding, not constant turmoil. You realize that true connection doesn't need drama to be deep and fulfilling. It's built on trust, consistency, and genuine affection - qualities often overshadowed by the drama.

Stepping Away

Making the decision to step away from a Drama Queen is tough but necessary for your well-being. It's about recognizing that you deserve peace and healthy relationships. This doesn't mean you don't care; it means you're prioritizing your mental and emotional health. It's a step towards finding relationships that uplift you, rather than drag you into an endless cycle of drama.

Craving Calm Waters

Eventually, the thrill of the drama loses its appeal, and you find yourself yearning for something more stable and serene. A relationship where disagreements don't escalate into melodramas and where peace isn't just the calm before another storm. You start to realize that genuine connections thrive on mutual respect, understanding, and quiet moments of intimacy – not endless episodes of conflict.

So, as you embark on your Valentine's Detox journey, think about what you really want from your relationships. It may be time to switch off the drama and find someone who's more about co-creating a love story based on mutual support, laughter, and those precious, drama-free moments together.

Spotting a Drama Queen: Imagine someone who can turn a spilled cup of coffee into a three-act tragedy. They've got a flair for the dramatic, making mountains out of molehills. They're the main character in every story, with a script full of woes, tragedies, and crises. It's like living with a reality TV star — except there's no off button. If you find yourself constantly embroiled in their latest catastrophe or tiptoeing around their emotional landmines, bingo — you've got a Drama Queen on your hands.

The Victim Player: Always the victim, they're experts at painting themselves as the perpetual underdog in every scenario. Every conversation is a new chapter in their saga of misfortunes, often embellished to gain more sympathy and attention from you.

The Crisis Creator: In a relationship with a Crisis Creator, there's never a dull moment, but for all the wrong reasons. They have a knack for turning minor disagreements into major crises. It's like they're addicted to the adrenaline of drama, and sadly, they expect you to play the hero every time.

The Gossip Monger: This partner thrives on the latest gossip and drama. Not only do they love being in the know, but they also enjoy adding fuel to the fire. They use gossip as a tool to remain at the center of attention and to manipulate the dynamics of the relationship.

The Overreactor: With them, every small issue becomes a major catastrophe. Misunderstandings or minor mishaps are blown out of proportion, often leading to unnecessary arguments and tension. It's their way of ensuring they remain the focus of your attention.

The Emotional Extortionist: This partner uses their emotions as leverage. Feelings of neglect or jealousy are often expressed through extreme emotional displays, from tears to tantrums, ensuring they become the center of your world again.

Detoxing from a Drama Queen

Okay, let's get strategic. First, build yourself an emotional fortress. You need to protect your peace. Engage with their dramas like you're a kindly but detached neighbor — supportive but not enmeshed. It's all about setting boundaries as sturdy as castle walls.

And remember, Drama Queens feed off reaction. So, the less you react, the less fuel they have for their fire. Encourage them to deal with issues head-on, without the need for an audience. It's like redirecting a child's tantrum — acknowledge the feelings but don't add to the drama. The idea is to establish a relationship environment where calm and stability are the norm, not the exception. It's like choosing to live in a serene countryside retreat instead of a bustling, noisy city. You're aiming for a relationship that feels like a cozy blanket, not a thunderstorm.

Being in a relationship with a Drama Queen requires a blend of compassion and firmness. It's about understanding their need for attention but not at the expense of your emotional well-being. Keep the drama for the movies and build a real-life love story that's more about mutual support and less about constant cliffhangers.

In short, detoxing from a Drama Queen is about creating a healthy balance. It's about learning to enjoy the show without becoming part of the script. So, grab your popcorn, observe, but remember — you're in the audience, not on stage.

BLAMER BONANZA

When talking about detoxing from relationships, the Blamers take center stage. They're the ones who never take responsibility for their actions.

These are the folks who've mastered the art of deflection. No matter the situation, somehow, it's never their fault. It's like living with a reverse Midas touch; everything they touch turns into a blame game instead of gold.

Blamers: The Masters of Deflection

Picture this: every time something goes wrong, no matter how small or big, a Blamer has their finger pointed outward. They're like escape artists, always finding a way out of taking responsibility. Trying to have a constructive conversation with them about issues in the relationship can feel like talking to a wall that talks back, insisting the wall on the other side is the problem.

The Blame Game on Valentine's Day

Valentine's Day, a time when love and partnership should be celebrated, can instead feel like walking through a minefield with a Blamer. You might find yourself on the receiving end of blame for not making the day special enough, or perhaps they'll find a way to make any mishaps your fault. It's draining, to say the least, and it can turn what should be a day of love into a day of tension and accusations.

The Impact of Constant Blaming

Living with constant blaming can take a toll on your self-esteem and mental health. It's challenging to grow and flourish in a relationship where your partner refuses to accept their share of responsibility. It breeds a toxic environment of mistrust and resentment. Instead of working together to solve problems, you're stuck in a loop of accusations and defensiveness.

Breaking Free from the Cycle

Recognizing the Blamer's behavior is the first step toward detoxing from this toxic relationship pattern. It's about understanding that you deserve a partner who can own up to their mistakes, who can work with you to build that metaphorical sandcastle without knocking it down with blame at every turn. Seeking a relationship built on mutual respect and accountability is key to finding genuine happiness and fulfillment.

Empowering Yourself

Empowering yourself in the face of a Blamer means setting clear boundaries and expressing your needs and feelings assertively. It's okay to demand a relationship where both partners can say, "I messed up, and I'm sorry," without fear of vulnerability being used as a weapon. It's about striving for a partnership where accountability is not just a one-way street but a shared journey towards growth and understanding.

In your Valentine's Detox, remember that detoxing from a Blamer is not just about removing negativity from your life. It's also about opening the door to relationships that are nurturing, where you can thrive together, acknowledging imperfections, and celebrating successes as a true team.

Spotting a Blamer: You know you're dealing with a Blamer when everything — and I mean everything — is always someone else's fault. Missed dinner plans? It's because of traffic, never their poor time management. Argument about chores? Obviously, it's because you're too demanding. They have this uncanny ability to twist situations so they're always the victim. It's like living with a human boomerang — everything you throw at them comes right back.

Here's a breakdown of the types of Blamers you might encounter:

The Perennial Finger-Pointer: Picture this: you're in a relationship where nothing is ever their fault. Plans didn't work out? It's because you didn't make them correctly. Misunderstanding in the relationship? Obviously, you misinterpreted their words. It's a pattern of shifting blame that leaves you perpetually frustrated and often questioning yourself.

The "It's Society's Fault" Pundit: This partner is an expert at dodging personal responsibility by blaming larger forces. It's not that they don't want to commit; it's society's skewed views on relationships. It's not their fault they're always late; it's the unrealistic expectations set by others. They use societal issues as a shield against personal accountability.

The Past-Dweller: This one's always living in the past. Their current relationship woes? All because of their ex or a rough upbringing. Instead of dealing with the present issues, they're stuck blaming past experiences, making it hard for the relationship to move forward.

The Complainer: Constant negativity is their game. No matter what you do, it's never right. Plan a surprise date? It's not what they wanted. Try to talk about improving the relationship? You're just pointing out their flaws. It's a never-ending cycle of complaints that can drain your energy.

The Injustice Collector: Ever been with someone who keeps a mental tally of every slight, real or imagined? They remember every forgotten anniversary, every misworded comment, and use these as ammunition in arguments. It's like they have a running scorecard, and unfortunately, you're always on the losing side.

Detoxing from a Blamer

First thing's first — keep communication as clear as crystal. When you talk to them about issues in the relationship, it's like navigating a minefield, so tread carefully but confidently. Let them know that in this two-player game, both need to hold the joystick.

Encourage them to leave their time machine and live in the here and now. Dwelling on past issues or mistakes doesn't do any good. It's about moving forward, not looking backward. And hey, setting boundaries is key. It's like drawing a line in the sand — it shows where your patience ends, and your self-respect begins.

Remember, you're aiming for a partnership, not a blame game. You deserve someone who stands with you, shoulder to shoulder, ready to face challenges together. It's about creating a relationship environment that's more like a team huddle and less like a courtroom drama.

Detoxing from someone who's always pointing the finger at you can be a bit of a tightrope walk. Especially if they're not on board with looking inward and doing the necessary soul-searching. Starting your detox often means taking a step back and creating some distance. Being the constant target of blame can really wear you down, messing with how you see yourself. You'll want to carve out your own space, surround yourself with folks who are all about that personal growth life. Find your squad, those who lift you up and reflect the kind of positive energy you need.

WANNABE WHINERS

Wannabes seem eternally stuck in a mindset of inadequacy and jealousy. They can't seem to shake off that feeling of never quite measuring up. When Valentine's rolls around, it's like their insecurities get a megaphone. Here's the lowdown on dealing with partners who've turned comparison into an art form and jealousy into their default mode.

The Constant Underdog

Ever feel like you're dating someone who's always playing the underdog? No matter what you do or say, they're stuck in this loop of feeling like they're always lagging behind everyone else. It's like being in a boat that's always taking on water, no matter how fast you bail it out. They're always looking over the fence, thinking everyone else's grass is greener, shinier, just... more.

Jealous Much?

And then there's the jealousy. Oh boy, does it get a workout around Valentine's Day. Every bouquet, every fancy dinner posted online is like a personal dig at them. It's exhausting, really. You're trying to enjoy your thing, but there's this constant buzz of "Why can't that be us?" or "See, they're doing it better." It's as if every other couple's highlight reel is a direct challenge to their self-esteem.

The Drain on Your Energy

Being with a Wannabe Energy Vampire is like being on emotional life support. You're always there, trying to pump them up, tell them they're good enough, smart enough, just enough. But it feels like a never-ending battle against their inner critic. The relationship starts feeling one-sided, with you playing cheerleader 24/7 while also trying to navigate your own stuff.

Spotting a Wannabe Energy Vampire

Spotting a Wannabe Energy Vampire: You can tell you're with a Wannabe when everything feels like a competition, but not the fun kind. Share an achievement, and they'll either one-up it or dismiss it. It's like playing a game they've rigged so you can't win. They're the masters of "Yeah, but..." — you know, "That's great, but when I did it..." or "That's cool, but it's not as good as...". It's exhausting because no matter what you do, it's never quite good enough for them. Here's the variety pack of Wannabe's.

The Chronic Comparer: These Energy Vampires are always measuring themselves against others. They constantly feel inadequate, even in the face of their successes. In a relationship, this can feel like you're always walking on eggshells, trying not to outshine them or trigger their insecurities.

The Buzzkill: Share a personal victory and watch them subtly deflate it. They struggle to genuinely celebrate your successes because it reflects on their self-imposed limitations. Your achievements become a mirror for what they believe they can't achieve, leading to a dampened atmosphere in the relationship.

The FOMO Fiend: Dating someone who's always worried they're missing out on something better can be exhausting. They're never fully present, always looking over the horizon for the next best thing. This constant restlessness can make building a stable, grounded relationship hard.

The Underachiever: In this case, your partner might avoid challenges, sticking to their comfort zone to avoid the risk of failure. This behavior can lead to a stagnant relationship, where growth and progress are sacrificed for the sake of playing it safe.

The Pity Party Host: They love to wallow in their despair, often turning every conversation into a session about their woes. They seek constant sympathy but reject solutions that might require them to change or take action.

~❖~

Dealing with a Wannabe in your love life can feel like you're in a relationship with a human raincloud when everyone's supposed to be all hearts and flowers. Wannabes have this knack for turning every silver lining into a grey cloud. You know the type: always comparing, always seeing the glass as half-empty, and just generally bringing down the mood.

Detoxing from a Wannabe

The Way Out? First off, it's about realizing that you can't be their only source of happiness or self-worth. They've got to find some of that mojo on their own. Encourage them to chase after what makes them tick, celebrate their wins, and maybe start seeing themselves as the champions you know they can be.

Building Them Up: Help them discover their own happy place. Maybe it's nudging them towards a new hobby or celebrating the small victories just as much as the big ones. It's about shifting the focus from what everyone else is doing to what they're achieving on their own terms. And yeah, it's about reminding them that the only person they should be competing with is who they were yesterday.

Moving Forward, Together

Getting through to a Wannabe takes patience and a whole lot of honest chats. Setting some ground rules, like not letting jealousy dictate the mood, and focusing on building each other up, can go a long way.

But what do you do when you're faced with a Wannabe who resists growth at every turn? It's a tough spot to be in. On one hand, you want to be supportive, encouraging them to see their own value and potential. But on the other hand, there's only so much you can do before it starts taking a toll on your own vibe.

Sacrificing your mental and emotional well-being in a bid to boost theirs isn't the answer. If every pep talk feels like shouting into the void, it might be time to draw a line. Remember, your responsibility is to your own growth and happiness. Sometimes, taking a break of separation or parting ways is the healthiest move, allowing both of you the space to find what truly fulfills you.

CRAB SHOWDOWN

You know how crabs in a bucket behave, right? If one tries to climb out and escape, the others pull it right back in. Well, this isn't just about crabs. It's spot-on for some relationships where one partner, driven by their own insecurities, constantly tries to pull the other down.

Picture this: a bunch of crabs in a bucket, one starts to climb out, reaching for freedom, and bam! The others grab hold and yank it back down. It's a wild scene. Now, imagine that scenario playing out in real life, but instead of crabs, it's you and your partner. You're trying to climb out of your metaphorical bucket, reaching for personal growth, new achievements, and a brighter, bigger version of your life. But every time you make a move, there's a tug that pulls you back. That's your

Crab Energy Vampire, clinging to their own fears and insecurities, determined to keep you in the bucket with them.

The Crab Bucket Syndrome

In relationships, the Crab Bucket Syndrome can be super subtle or glaringly obvious. It's like every time you're on the verge of something great, there's a comment, a look, or an action from your partner that just saps the joy right out of it. Maybe you landed a promotion, and instead of popping the champagne, it's met with a, "Who's gonna make dinner if you're always working late?" Or you're excited about a new fitness goal, and you get hit with a, "Why bother? You look fine as you are." It's not just about keeping you in place; it's about them feeling safe in the familiarity of the bucket.

Cracking the Crab Mentality

Dealing with this mentality is tricky. It's like a dance where you're constantly trying to move forward, but your partner's steps are all about pulling you back. The key? It's understanding the dance itself. Your partner's fear of losing you or of change itself might be driving their actions. It's tough because, on one hand, you love them, but on the other, you've got this burning desire to grow, to evolve, and to break free from the bucket.

The Tug-of-War: When They Pull You Back

It's like every step you take towards something positive, they've got a reason why it won't work or why you shouldn't bother. Maybe they're scared of being left behind or maybe they just can't stand to see someone else shining too bright. Whatever the reason, it's exhausting. You're trying to grow, to reach for more, but every move is met with negativity, doubt, and sometimes, outright sabotage.

Now let's look at a sample of these Crab Energy Vampires

The Competitive Underminer: They freely give backhanded compliments? They say something nice, then sneak in a little dig, followed by another vague nicety. They're crafty at subtly undercutting your confidence while pretending to be supportive. It's their way of keeping you off balance.

The Spotlight Stealer: This partner can't stand to see you shine. Achieve something great, and watch them shift the focus to themselves, often by creating a scene. It's like they need to be the center of attention, even if it means overshadowing your accomplishments.

The Chronic Criticizer: Nothing you do is ever quite right for them. They have a remark or 'helpful' criticism for everything, from the way you dress to how you handle your work. It's a constant drip of negativity, wearing away at your self-esteem.

The Emotional Guilt-Tripper: Feel like you're being emotionally blackmailed? That's them. They use guilt to manipulate you into staying close, making you feel responsible for their emotional well-being. It's a tactic to keep you tethered to their side, playing on your sympathies.

The Drama Instigator: They love to stir the pot and watch the chaos unfold. It's like they get a thrill from setting people against each other, then sitting back to watch the drama. It's a diversion tactic, drawing attention away from their insecurities by creating turmoil around them.

The Win-Lose Outlook: Partners playing the crab role often see the relationship as a win-lose scenario. Every time their significant other gets a win — be it a new job, a hobby, or just a good day — they see it as their own loss. It's a constant battle, and in their eyes, their partner's gain is their loss.

How They Pull You Down: The methods can be pretty sneaky. Sometimes it's the small stuff, like a sarcastic comment or a passive-aggressive jibe. Other times, it's more direct — like discouragement, emotional manipulation, or guilt trips. They might downplay your successes, brush off your ambitions, or even isolate you from people who support you.

In the Grip of Insecurity: In these scenarios, you've got one partner who's like the crab reaching for the rim of the bucket, aiming for something better or just trying to be happy. The other partner, bogged down by insecurity, acts like those crabs at the bottom, tugging them back. It's a reflection of their own fears and doubts, where they disrupt their partner's attempts to grow or find joy. It's as if they're thinking, "If I can't be happy, neither can you."

The Effect on Your Growth: This kind of relationship can really stunt your growth and chip away at your self-esteem. Imagine being on the verge of something awesome, only to have your partner drag you back with their negativity. Over time, this can lead to feeling unworthy and stuck, not just in the relationship, but in life too.

Detoxing from a Crab

This is where you need to be like a ninja with your boundaries. Imagine drawing a line in the sand with a big, fat marker. It's about knowing where you end, and they begin. When they start their usual undermining tactics, call it out. Not in a confrontational way, but more like, "I see what you did there, and I'm not playing along." Keep the communication open and honest, but don't get sucked into their drama.

It's like you're building an emotional fortress around yourself, not to keep them out, but to keep your sanity in. A healthy relationship is a two-way street, not a one-way guilt trip. Encourage them to share their insecurities in a healthy way, instead of using them as weapons.

Bucket Conversations

The first step to getting out of this is recognizing what's happening. Understand that their behavior says more about their insecurities than your worth. Setting boundaries is key, and so is having clear conversations about what's okay and what's not.

Focus on empowering yourself. Your achievements and happiness are important. Make sure you're surrounded by people who lift you up and encourage you, not those who try to drag you down.

Sometimes, the healthiest thing to do is to step away from the relationship, especially if it's become toxic and resistant to change. Prioritize your well-being and your growth. Choose to step out of the bucket if that's what it takes to move forward.

Choosing Your Path

Remember, relationships should be about support, love, and growing together, not a constant struggle for dominance. If you find yourself in a crab bucket situation, don't be afraid to reach for the top. True love and support will never try to clip your wings; it will be the wind that helps you soar.

When you're tangled up with a Crab energy vampire, it can feel like you're in a love story penned by someone with a really twisted sense of humor. Crabs are the partners with a doctorate in undermining and manipulation. They're like emotional quicksand — the more you try to please them, the deeper you sink.

Escaping the Bucket

So, what's the move? First off, recognizing that you're in a bucket is a big step. Next up, it's about figuring out if your partner is willing to climb out with you or if they're set on staying put, anchored by their insecurities. Sometimes, a good heart-to-heart can shed light on the situation, offering them a rope to climb out with you. But if they're just not budging, if every attempt at growth is met with resistance, it might be time to make a solo climb. It's not about abandoning ship (or bucket, in this case); it's about realizing that your journey to personal growth might need to be a solo mission.

Remember, the goal isn't to escape and leave everyone behind; it's about finding that balance where you can grow without being pulled back. Sometimes, the bravest thing you can do is to keep climbing, offering a hand, hoping they'll join you. But always know that your journey upwards is valuable, and your place isn't stuck at the bottom of a bucket, no matter how familiar it may feel.

VICTIM PITY PARTY

Imagine you're in a relationship where every day feels like a rerun of the same sad story. Your partner, a classic Victim-type energy vampire, always seems to be dealing with some drama or misfortune. You find yourself constantly in the role of the hero, the one who's expected to lift their spirits or solve their endless string of problems. It's like you're co-starring in their never-ending personal drama series, where they're always the victim, and you? You're the designated savior.

Spotting the Victim: It's like having a personal alert for every tiny mishap in their life. Missed the bus? Crisis. Spilled coffee? Tragedy. They've got a talent for turning molehills into mountains, and guess who's expected to climb them? Yep, you. It's not just about lending an ear; it's like being their emotional lifeline. If you find yourself more in the role of a counselor than a partner, that's your cue. Healthy relationships are about mutual support, not an endless rescue mission.

This Victim-type has mastered the art of being the perpetual sufferer. They've got this narrative down pat, portraying themselves as the ones who are always wronged, forever stuck in a loop of complaints and self-pity. They're experts at drawing sympathy, often manipulating those around them into becoming their caregivers or problem-solvers.

Being in a relationship with a Victim can skew the balance significantly. You might feel like it's your sole responsibility to ensure their happiness and well-being. This dynamic often leads to a lopsided relationship, where you're putting in all the effort to 'fix' them, which can be incredibly draining on your emotional reserves.

Here's the thing — it's an emotional vortex. In this setup, you end up feeling exhausted, as if an emotional void is swallowing all your efforts. The relationship starts to feel more like a therapeutic session or a caretaking role, rather than a partnership. It's a one-sided emotional labor, with you constantly giving and them perpetually taking.

Here's what the world of the Victim Energy Vampire looks like

The Constant Complainer: They have a PhD in complaining. Everything's always wrong — the weather's too this, their job's too that. Every chat with them turns into a vent session, and you? You're trying to be the cheer squad, offering solutions that never stick. It's like pouring your energy into a bottomless pit, and boy, is it draining.

The Perpetual Pessimist: Picture this: You're having a great day, but your partner? They've got a knack for finding that dark cloud on a sunny day. It's all doom and gloom, all the time. Trying to bring some sunshine into their life can feel like you're pushing a boulder uphill, and it's exhausting.

The Drama Magnet: Some people attract drama like magnets, right? If you're with a Drama Magnet, you're probably used to being in crisis mode. There's always some disaster happening around them, and guess who's expected to play superhero? Yep, you. It's tiring, always being on crisis control, and it really takes a toll on your time together.

The Guilt Tripper: Sneaky and subtle, the Guilt Tripper knows just how to pull those heartstrings. They've got a whole arsenal of "remember when I..." or "my life is so tough because...". Before you know it, you're feeling like you owe them the world. It's a clever form of manipulation that can leave you feeling like you're stuck in emotional quicksand, always trying to make things right for them.

Victim Energy Vampires can make you feel like you're constantly stuck in 'saving' mode. This type of partner is all about the drama of their woes, and somehow, you end up being cast as the hero in their never-ending saga of despair.

So, as you navigate your Valentine's Detox journey, breaking free from a Victim-type partner involves recognizing this unhealthy pattern. Understand that it's not your duty to be their perpetual happiness provider or problem solver. Yes, it's good to be supportive, but becoming their emotional lifeline is not healthy. A balanced relationship is about mutual support and upliftment, where both partners contribute equally rather than one shouldering all the emotional work.

Detox Strategy: Picture setting boundaries like building a moat around your emotional castle. It's not about cutting them off but protecting your space. When they start spinning their tales of woe, listen, but don't dive into the drama. Encourage them to find solutions instead of wallowing. If they start playing the blame game, gently steer them towards taking responsibility. This is about fostering a relationship where both partners stand on their own two feet, offering support without becoming an emotional crutch.

Detoxing from a Victim Energy Vampire is about working toward a partnership that thrives on equality and mutual respect, not dependency. It's about creating a space where both of you can grow, not just one person always doing the heavy emotional lifting. If boundaries and honest communication don't work and they are not willing to develop to become more of a drama-free human, you may find yourself in a self-rescue situation, looking for your parachute and the exit.

THE CONTROLLER CONUNDRUM

Alright, let's dive into the world of "The Controller" in relationships, especially when you're on that path of Valentine's Detox and looking to free yourself from toxic dynamics. Picture being with someone who always needs to be in the driver's seat, not just literally, but in every aspect of the relationship.

These Energy Vampires act like they've got a monopoly on the truth. They're the type who think their way is the only way. Controllers are like those strict teachers from school who wouldn't tolerate a speck of dust out of place. They're all about order, perfection, and, well, control.

In a relationship with a Controller, you might feel like you're living under a microscope. They've got an opinion on everything — how you dress, talk, and even what you should be thinking. It's like walking a tightrope, where one wrong step means a barrage of criticism or a long lecture on how you could've done it 'their way.'

Spotting the Controller

The Upper hand Game: Do you find yourself second-guessing your choices because of what your partner might think? Changing your clothes, ditching friends, or dropping hobbies to avoid their disapproval? That's classic Controller avoidance behavior. They love to have the upper hand in everything, from what you wear to who you hang out with. Slowly, you might feel like you're losing pieces of yourself, molding into the person they want you to be rather than who you really are. Here are a few of the masks of the Controller.

The Micromanager: This type of Controller has an eye for detail, but not in a good way. They want to oversee every little aspect of your life. From how you fold your laundry to the friends you choose, they have a say in it all. Being with a Micromanager can feel suffocating like you're living under a constant magnifying glass.

The Opinion Enforcer: Meet the Controller who believes their opinions are gospel truth. They have a black-and-white view of the world, and anything that doesn't align with their beliefs is wrong. In a relationship, this can look like them trying to reshape your beliefs and opinions to match theirs, leaving little room for individual thought or expression.

The Planner: This Controller loves to have a plan for everything, and spontaneity is a big no-no. Every date, every weekend, every life goal must be meticulously planned out. While being organized is great, with the Planner, it often means their plan is the only one that matters. Deviating from their script can lead to conflict or outright dismissal of your ideas.

~ ❖ ~

Dealing with a Controller in your relationship, especially when Valentine's Day is looming, can make you feel like you're living under constant scrutiny. It's as though every choice you make needs their thumbs-up. Imagine your life as a movie, and there's this person who insists on directing every scene. But remember, you're not just playing a role here. You have your own story to live and tell.

Taking Back the Helm: Think of yourself as the captain of your own ship. It's high time you took control of the steering wheel. Begin by drawing clear lines in the sand about what's off-limits—your personal choices, your alone time, your freedom to be you. It's crucial to have that frank discussion, making it crystal clear: "This is who I am, take it or leave it." However, remember it takes two to tango. They've got to be willing to respect your individuality. If that's not in the cards, you might need to consider whether this relationship is more about dominance than partnership.

The Detox Plan: Breaking free from a Controller means taking back your identity and ensuring your relationship is a two-way street of mutual respect and freedom. Keep in mind, you're not on the lookout for someone to 'complete' you—you're complete by yourself. What you need is a co-pilot, not someone trying to take over the flight controls. So, hold firm, stay true to who you are, and aim for a relationship that values and celebrates your unique self.

BULLY IN THE LOVE LANE

We've all heard about bullies in the schoolyard, but what about the relationship bullies? You know, those partners who seem to have taken a few too many pointers from high school bullies.

Picture this: You're all set for a cozy Valentine's Day, thinking it's all about heart-shaped chocolates and those cute little cards. But then, boom, you're suddenly dealing with a partner who acts like everything is about them. It feels like you're back in the schoolyard facing off against the class bully. They've got this way of making everything a flex, using their words or actions to push you around emotionally.

It's like they get their kicks from making you feel small or insignificant. They're more about power plays than bouquets. Every day is a tug-of-war, and you're always on the losing side. Yeah, they're real, and they can turn what's supposed to be a love story into a bit of a horror flick.

Meet the Bully…

Mr. or Ms. Intimidator: This one's all about flexing their muscles, not literally (well, sometimes literally), but more in the way they talk and act. They've got this vibe that says, 'Do it my way, or else.' It's not about physical threats, but more like they're playing mind games to keep you in check.

The Sneaky Belittler: Oh, they're crafty. They'll throw a compliment your way, but it's wrapped in a zinger that leaves you feeling about two inches tall. It's their way of keeping you guessing — are they sweet or just plain sour?

Wordsmith Warrior: Their weapon of choice? Words. And they're not the lovey-dovey kind. We're talking sharp, cutting, and sometimes downright brutal. They turn arguments into art forms and not the pretty kind.

Navigating the Storm: Dealing with a bully in your love life is like trying to sail through a hurricane. When you think it's all clear skies and smooth sailing, they whip up a storm that leaves you reeling.

~ ~

Recognizing you're with a bully isn't always easy, especially when you're wearing those rose-colored glasses. But it's all about how you feel — are you constantly on edge, feeling put down, or like you're never quite good enough? That's your cue.

Detox Time: Alright, so how do you detox from a bully in your love life? First, it's about standing up for yourself. You've got to steer away from those rocky shores. Set your boundaries — make it clear what's cool and what's absolutely not.

If talking it out doesn't work, it might be time to rethink the whole relationship. Remember, love is supposed to lift you up, not drag you down into the depths of despair. It's about mutual respect, not one person calling all the shots.

THE PERPETUAL CRITIC

Imagine this: You're trying to find peace and positivity, but there's 'The Critic' in your life, always ready with a harsh word or a disapproving glance. This isn't just about nitpicking; it's about how their constant criticism can make you feel trapped and undervalued in a relationship that's supposed to be about love and support.

Recognizing The Critic

No matter what you do, it's never quite good enough for them? That's a big red flag. Critics love to focus on flaws, often overlooking the good stuff. Their criticism doesn't come from a place of wanting to help you grow; it's more about keeping you small and under their thumb. This constant negative feedback can leave you feeling deflated and unde-serving.

The Nitpicker: This person zeroes in on every small flaw or mistake. It's like they can't help but point out everything they think you're doing wrong. This constant criticism can make you feel like you're walking on eggshells, always anxious about making a mistake.

The "Never Good Enough" Coach: With them, your best efforts are never enough. They set impossibly high standards, and no matter how hard you try, you can never seem to meet them. This can lead to feelings of inadequacy and low self-esteem.

The "Honesty Brutalist": They mask their hurtful comments under the guise of 'just being honest,' but their words can be cutting and de-moralizing. They often dismiss your feelings, saying you're too sensitive or can't take a joke.

'The Critic' in a relationship can feel like you're always under a harsh spotlight. They have a way of zeroing in on your flaws, and every cri-tique feels like a sharp jab rather than a helping hand. It's like they have a magnifying glass on your every move, quick to point out what you did wrong but slow to celebrate what you do right.

Detox Strategy: Time to pump up your self-esteem and remember who you are. The Critic's words are a reflection of their issues, not yours. Start by having a heart-to-heart, letting them know how their words affect you. Draw your lines in the sand — what you're okay with and what's absolutely off-limits. If they can't respect that, then it might be a cue for you to reassess the relationship. You're in the market for a cheerleader, not a critic.

Detoxing from a Critic: This is about building a fortress of self-love and recognizing your worth. It's understanding that constructive feed-back is one thing, but constant criticism is another ball game altogether. You deserve someone who celebrates your strengths and supports you through your weaknesses, not someone who uses them as ammunition. Here's to finding a love that lifts you up, not one that keeps you down.

EMOTIONAL BAND-AIDS

Alright, let's shine a light on something we often overlook—those sneaky little things called Emotional Band-Aids. You know, those quick-fix habits or maybe those 'just one more' clicks on the online shopping spree we dive into when we're feeling a bit low or empty.

These are the little habits and fixes we lean on when navigating the rocky terrain of toxic relationships or dealing with the emotional voids left behind. They're like those quick-fix solutions we grab in a pinch, not really solving the problem but giving us temporary relief.

Imagine this: Valentine's Day is rolling around, and instead of feeling all loved up, you're reaching for that extra slice of cake, binge-watching your favorite show till 3 AM, or maybe drowning in the endless scroll of social media. It's like we're trying to patch up an emotional void with stuff that doesn't stick.

Here's a few of those familiar Band-Aids…

The Comfort Food Consumer

Picture this: a rough day ends with you, a couch, and a giant tub of ice cream. Sounds familiar? That's the classic Comfort Food Consumer. They turn to food, especially the comforting but unhealthy kind, to soothe emotional aches. It's a sweet escape but often leaves you feeling physically and emotionally drained afterward.

The Retail Therapy Addict

Shopping is more than a spree; it's a coping mechanism. Picking up something shiny and new offers a momentary buzz, a distraction from deeper feelings of inadequacy or sadness. But the high fades quickly, often replaced by guilt or anxiety about spending.

The Social Media Scroller

This one lives for the 'likes' and online validation. Social media becomes a measuring stick for their self-esteem. But it's a trap because they also end up comparing their real life to everyone else's curated online personas, spiraling into feelings of not being good enough.

The News Junkie

Here's the person who's glued to the news feed, constantly updating themselves on every twist and turn in current events. It gives them a sense of control, but ironically, it often heightens their anxiety and stress, trapping them in a cycle of information overload.

The Serial Dater

Afraid of being alone, they jump from one relationship to the next. Each new partner is like a Band-Aid over a wound that needs time to heal. They're searching for someone to fill the emptiness, but it's a journey that needs to start from within.

The Jack-of-All-Triggers

This type is always on the lookout for the next distraction — binge-watching, impulsive shopping, you name it. Anything to avoid facing the deeper feelings of emptiness or inadequacy that haunt them.

So, when we talk about these Emotional Band-Aids, think of them as those quick fixes we rely on when we're feeling a bit down. You know, like diving into a tub of ice cream or going on a shopping spree. But here's the deal - they're like Band-Aids over a wound. They give us some relief in the moment, but they don't really tackle the deeper emotional stuff. Whether it's comfort food, retail therapy, seeking likes on social media, staying glued to the news, hopping from one relationship to another, or constantly finding distractions, they're not the real solution. It's time to recognize them for what they are and think about a more genuine way to heal those emotional wounds.

WHICH WAY DO YOU GO?

So, you're in a relationship, and you are all about personal growth and moving forward, but your partner? They're just not on the same page. They resist change, hold on to their old ways, and seem content to stay right where they are. It's like you're trying to climb a mountain, and they're all comfortable camping at base camp forever.

Now, it's a bit of a sticky situation, right? On one hand, you care about them, maybe even love them. On the other hand, you've got your own mental and emotional well-being to consider. It's like standing at a crossroads, with one sign saying, "Sacrifice your happiness for the sake of keeping the peace," and the other sign pointing towards the possibility of parting ways to nurture your own growth.

So, what do you do when they're resisting growth? Do you keep pushing, hoping they'll catch up, or do you accept that your paths might be going in different directions? It's not about giving up at the first sign of resistance. People need time to adjust, understand, and make their own moves toward change. But it's also important to recognize when the resistance isn't just a phase; it's their conscious choice.

Now, sacrificing your own mental and emotional health isn't some heroic act as it's sometimes portrayed. It's like trying to fill someone else's cup while yours is leaking; sooner or later, you're going to run dry. And let's face it, a relationship where one person is constantly trying to 'fix' or change the other? That's not a partnership; that's a full-blown project.

So, when do you draw the line? Well, it's when you realize that your journey towards growth is getting blocked by staying together. It's when the thought of parting ways feels less like a loss and more like a necessary step toward your own well-being. It's definitely a tough call, no doubt about it. But it's also about respecting yourself and your partner enough to understand that sometimes love isn't about holding on; it's about letting go.

Now, breaking up doesn't have to be some dramatic showdown. It can be a mutual understanding that you're both headed in different directions, and that's perfectly fine. It's about wishing each other well on your separate journeys, even if those journeys aren't intertwined anymore. At the end of the day, your mental and emotional health should be your top priority. Choosing a path that nurtures that isn't selfish—it's necessary. And who knows? Sometimes, it's the act of letting go that finally encourages growth, both for you and your partner.

YOUR NAGGING INNER VAMPIRE

Sometimes, the biggest battles we face aren't with the world outside but with those sneaky little doubts and negative self-talk lurking in our minds. We're talking about our very own Inner Vampire, that nagging voice that loves to tell us we're just not good enough for love or anything else great. But here's the scoop. We're going to tackle this head-on and turn that inner critic into our biggest cheerleader.

Understanding The Inner Vampire

What's this Inner Vampire all about? It's like having a personal critic living rent-free in your head, always ready with a snide comment or a reminder of your past mistakes. This little monster feeds on our deepest insecurities, whispering that we're unworthy of love or destined to repeat our relationship blunders.

But where does this come from? It's a cocktail of past experiences, maybe a critical parent, a tough breakup, or just the pressure cooker of society's expectations. These experiences plant seeds of doubt that grow into our Inner Vampire, coloring how we see ourselves and the world.

Alright, let's dive a bit deeper into the concept of our Inner Vampire. Imagine this: inside your head, there's this little creature, your own personal critic, who's got a knack for highlighting your every flaw, mistake, and fear. It thrives on your insecurities, constantly whispering things like, "You're not good enough," "You'll just mess it up again," or "Who would love someone like you?" This is your Inner Vampire, the embodiment of toxic thoughts, self-doubt, low self-esteem, and all those fears that hold you back.

Now, where does this pesky critter come from? It's not like you wake up one day, and boom, there it is. No, it's more subtle than that. This Inner Vampire is often born from a mix of past experiences. Maybe you had a parent who was a bit too critical, a relationship that left you doubting your worth, or perhaps it's the relentless pressure from society to be perfect.

The self-doubt fed from our Inner Vampire is also good at keeping us in a loop of negativity, and they are the bait for getting stuck in relationships that do more harm than good.

When we're constantly beating ourselves up with thoughts like, "Is this really as good as it gets?" or "Am I even worthy of something better?" it's like we're rolling out the red carpet for these vampires, inviting them to stick around and mess with us.

Our inner Vampire loves to feast on our insecurities, making us believe we're not cut out for love, respect, or happiness. They've got us thinking that staying in a bad relationship is less scary than breaking free and starting fresh. It's like we're trapped in our own heads, convinced that moving on is just too big of a leap.

But guess what? We've got more power over these shadowy figures than we think. It all begins with calling their bluff, questioning the doom-and-gloom stories they've been feeding us.

Do any of these Inner Vampire vibes sound familiar to you?

The Perfectionist Predator: This version of our Inner Vampire is all about perfection. It lurks in the shadows of our achievements, always pointing out the flaws, no matter how small. Finished a project at work? "It could have been better," it hisses. Managed to hit your fitness goal? "But did you see how much better everyone else is doing?" it sneers. This Perfectionist Predator sets impossibly high standards, ensuring you're always falling short in its eyes, fueling a never-ending cycle of self-doubt and dissatisfaction.

The Fear Feaster: Ever felt paralyzed by fear, unable to take even the smallest step toward your goals? That's the Fear Feaster at work. It thrives on your anxieties, feasting on every "what if" scenario you can conjure up. Planning to ask for a raise? "What if you get rejected?" it whispers. Thinking about starting a new relationship? "Remember how the last one ended," it reminds you. The Fear Feaster loves to keep you in a state of inaction, always scared of what might go wrong.

The Regret Reaper: The Regret Reaper is a sneaky one. It digs up your past mistakes and failures, no matter how deeply you've buried them. This Inner Vampire doesn't want you to forget about that embarrassing thing you said five years ago or the opportunity you missed because you were too hesitant. "You always mess up," it taunts, keeping you chained to your past and doubtful of your ability to make better decisions in the future.

The Validation Vampire: This people-pleasing Vampire is particularly cunning, feeding on your need for approval and acceptance from others. This Inner Vampire convinces you that your worth is determined solely by what others think of you. "Did they like your presentation, or were they just being polite?" it questions. "If you don't attend that event, everyone will think less of you," it warns. This vampire drives you to exhaust yourself in the pursuit of pleasing everyone, leaving little room for self-care or understanding your own needs and desires. It thrives on your fear of rejection, keeping you in a constant state of anxiety over potentially disappointing others.

The Validation Vampire's power diminishes as you start to recognize your intrinsic value, independent of external validation. Learning to love and accept yourself, flaws and all, is its kryptonite. By establishing boundaries, prioritizing self-care, and embracing your authentic self, you begin to starve this vampire of its power. As you learn self-love and acceptance, you'll find that the need for constant approval fades, and the voice of the Validation Vampire becomes a distant whisper, overshadowed by your own inner strength and self-assurance.

These Inner Vampires have a knack for sneaking up on us, subtly undermining our confidence and nibbling away at our happiness. But here's the game changer: spotting them. It's like flipping on the kitchen light and seeing the roaches scatter. Suddenly, you know exactly what you're dealing with.

Once you've got them in your sights, it's time to get a little confrontational. Start poking holes in their arguments. When they whisper, "You're not good enough," hit back with, "Says who?" Challenge them and demand evidence. Spoiler alert: they won't have any because, let's face it, that's all just BS.

And here's a crucial piece: be kind to yourself. This isn't about beating yourself up for listening to them in the first place. It's about recognizing you're human, and these doubts are as common as dirt but far less useful.

As you get better at this—questioning the validity of those vampires' whispers, seeking out the real truths, and practicing a bit of self-love—something good happens. Those once-menacing vampires start to shrink. They become less of this overwhelming force and more like that annoying background noise you can tune out, like a distant car alarm or the hum of a fridge. Eventually, they're just part of the scenery of your mind, noticeable but not capable of throwing you off your game.

As we peel back the layers of our Inner Vampires—be it the Perfectionist Predator, the Fear Feaster, the Regret Reaper, or the Validation Vampire—a common thread emerges, we are the culprits that invite them into our lives with our self-talk. These vampires don't just materialize out of thin air; they are, in essence, born from and nourished by the conversation in our minds.

More often than not, our Inner Vampire is something we create with the questions we ask ourselves. These questions act like seeds of doubt that, over time, grow into this critical voice that colors your view of yourself and the world around you. It's like we're feeding this vampire with the negative questions we ask ourselves, allowing it to grow stronger.

The questions we pose to ourselves—without even realizing it—can either give us power or give these vampires more room to haunt our thoughts.

When we ask ourselves, "Why do I always fail?" or "What's wrong with me?" we invite these vampires to the table, offering them a feast of doubts and fears. In these moments of self-questioning, our Inner Vampires find their strength, growing bolder with every negative inquiry that echoes through the chambers of our minds.

Recognizing this link between our self-interrogations and the power of our Inner Vampires is the first step towards turning the tables, transforming these shadowy tormentors into silent whispers of the past.

INNER VAMPIRE QUESTIONS

Have you ever felt stuck in a never-ending loop of not-so-great relationships? It's like there's this sneaky little trickster in our minds, always asking questions that keep us bogged down in the muck. Here's a thought: what if the secret key to breaking free from toxic love is, in fact, the very questions we ask ourselves?

Our love story is like a living tale of how we view the world and the questions we've been asking. Questions are like spells that we cast on ourselves. They are magnets drawing us closer to the preview of coming attractions for our lives. They can either jazz up our journey or keep us stuck in the same old relationship ruts.

It's like we are wizards of our own world, casting these spells without even realizing it. And if our mental playlist is jam-packed with downer questions, we're practically enchanting ourselves into a repeat cycle of love mishaps.

If your default question is, "Why do I always end up with the wrong person?" your brain will throw a pity party and list all the reasons. It's like ordering a dish you know you don't like and then wondering why you're not enjoying the meal. But here's where the magic happens: you can change your order. Start asking yourself questions like, "What can I do to attract the kind of love that feels right?" and voila — you're changing your story by giving your brain a brand-new mission.

Think of these empowering questions as seeds you're planting in your mental garden. They set the stage for what's to come and guide your choices. When we start tossing around questions that match the love story we're itching to live, we begin to make choices that nudge us in that direction. It's like plugging in a new destination in your GPS and following the route it suggests.

But remember, changing your story is not a one-and-done deal. It's about making positive questions a regular habit in your daily thought concert. We're talking about tuning your inner radio to a station that plays all the greatest hits of self-love, respect, and positive vibes.

So, as we move through this journey of detoxing from the not-so-great love connections, let's change our story by remixing our questions. Let's swap the "Why can't I find love?" with "What makes me an absolute catch?" or turn "Why do my relationships fizzle out?" into "How can I spark a relationship that's all about trust and respect?" Let's ask ourselves the good stuff, the questions that light up our love life like a fireworks show.

By switching up our questions, we redirect our focus and reshape our story. It's like setting a new course on our love life's GPS. This kind of shift brings about a transformation that goes beyond our romantic endeavors; it influences our entire approach to life. It's about breaking free from the orbit of self-doubt and propelling ourselves into a universe of empowerment and positive vibes. It's time to ask those empowering questions that steer us toward the love story we're truly meant to live — one filled with self-respect, joy, and the kind of love that we not only desire but truly deserve.

Better Questions...

Our brains are these amazing, answer-generating machines. Ask them a question, any question, and they'll work overtime to find an answer. But here's the catch — if you're constantly throwing negative questions at your brain, like "Why do I always end up in bad relationships?" or "What's wrong with me?", your brain's going to serve up answers that validate these negative thoughts. It's like ordering the same unfulfilling dish from life's menu over and over again and expecting it will taste better each time.

But what if we switch up the menu? Start asking ourselves empowering questions that uplift and inspire us, like:

"How can I snag a healthy relationship?" or "What makes me a total catch?" Suddenly, your brain's whipping up a whole new batch of answers, ones that might scoot you out of the toxic relationship loop and into something way better.

Have you ever caught yourself with these kinds of downers?

1. Feeling like you're not love material?
2. Wondering what's so wrong with you that love's a no-show?
3. Pushing away the good ones without knowing why?

Let's flip those into something a bit more upbeat:

1. What's so awesome about me that makes me deserving of love?
2. How can I amp up the self-love and draw in some great relationships?
3. How can I open up and let the good vibes and people in?

These kinds of questions put you in the driver's seat, focusing on growth and the good stuff. And, hey, here are a few more of those not-so-helpful thoughts:

"Why's it so hard to find someone?"

"Why do all my relationships crash and burn?"

"What's the deal with me still being single?"

"Why am I a magnet for the wrong crowd?"

"Why's no one getting me?"

"Why's it always me getting hurt?"

"Why do I feel so unlovable?"

"Am I going solo for good?"

"Why's love gotta be so complicated?"

Now, let's tweak those into questions that give you a boost:

"How can I better connect with and attract my kind of person?"

"What have my past flings taught me for healthier future ones?"

"What makes me stand out, single and all?"

"How do I line up my vibe to attract the right crowd?

"How can I get my feelings and needs across better?"

"What can I do to set up some solid boundaries for my well-being?"

"In what ways am I totally lovable?"

"How can I make my future relationships simpler and sweeter?"

Switching from those negative questions to positive ones is like high-fiving your love life. It's about getting pumped for the best version of your love journey. Remember, the energy you radiate is the love you're inviting in.

It's a game-changer to switch up the internal chat. Instead of letting the gloomy questions keep you in a loop of doubt and crummy relationships, start quizzing yourself with stuff that frees and fires you up. These positive questions unlock new paths filled with self-respect, a solid sense of self, and way healthier connections. This isn't just about love; it works for everything in life.

Think about it. When you're knee-deep in the muck of a toxic relationship, it's like you're wearing these heavy boots made of doubts and fears. And the crazy part? The laces are tied up with all these tricky questions we keep asking ourselves. It's a real tangle.

Why do I always fall for the wrong one?

What's wrong with me?

These questions are like walking in circles in those heavy boots — you don't get anywhere and end up feeling more stuck.

But what if we switch out those heavy boots for something lighter? Imagine slipping on a pair of those snazzy sneakers that make you feel like you can run a marathon or dance all night. That's what happens when you start asking yourself empowering questions. How can I make my love life healthier? What do I really deserve from a partner? It's like these questions have springs in them, bouncing you out of the toxic loop and into a whole new rhythm.

Let's face it, we've all been there, where our inner dialogue sounds more like a broken record of doom and gloom. But here's a secret — flip the script, and it changes the whole dance. Instead of asking why you're stuck in this bad romance, ask what steps you can take to cha-cha your way out of it. It's about setting the tone for a new tune, one where you're the DJ, mixing in beats of self-love, confidence, and a dash of sass.

So, hit pause the next time you catch yourself spiraling down that rabbit hole of self-doubt and toxic questioning. Change the script. Ask yourself something to lift you up, set your soul on fire, and get those positive vibes flowing. It's all about the questions. They're the secret ingredient in your life's soundtrack. Choose the ones that make you feel like you're the star of your own show, strutting down the path of a life filled with healthier relationships and a whole lot of self-respect.

It's not just about finding new answers; it's about asking better questions. Because when you start doing that, you're not just changing the conversation — you're changing the game. And that is where your journey to a Valentine's Detox from toxic relationships truly begins.

Bottom line? The questions you ask yourself can be your dance floor or your quicksand. Choose the ones that make you feel like dancing. Because trust me, once you start grooving to the rhythm of empowering questions, you'll wonder why you ever settled for that old toxic playlist.

Questions are Assumptions

When immersed in the choppy waters of relationships or just life in general, the questions we toss around in our heads are more than just idle thoughts. They're like the architects of our expectations, building up the world we expect to live in.

Think about it: when you ask yourself, "Why do I always end up in bad relationships?" you're not just musing over your love life; you're setting up an expectation based on the assumption that you're doomed to repeat the pattern.

These questions, they're sneaky. They slip in assumptions as if they're facts, painting our outlook with colors we didn't even choose. It's as if by asking, "What's wrong with me?" we're assuming there is something inherently wrong, to begin with. Our brains, bless them, are hardwired to answer the questions we ask, no matter how they're framed. So, when we base our questions on negative assumptions, we set ourselves up to see the world through a lens tinted with doubt and self-criticism.

But here's where the magic happens: when we start tweaking those questions. Instead of asking why things always go south, what if we ask, "How can I open myself up to healthier relationships?" or "What have I learned from my past that can guide me toward something better?" Suddenly, the assumptions shift. We're no longer assuming the worst; we're opening the door to growth and positive change. Our expectations start to realign, too. We're not just hoping to dodge another toxic relationship; we're actively looking for ways to foster something meaningful and nourishing.

These empowering questions don't just challenge our assumptions; they rewrite them. They remind us that we're not stuck in a narrative unless we choose to be. By asking questions that assume our strength, resilience, and worth, we're not only expecting better outcomes; we're setting the stage for them. It's like shifting from expecting another re-run of the same old sitcom to anticipating a blockbuster movie premiere. The storyline changes, the characters develop, and suddenly, you're not just a spectator in your life but the star.

So, next time you catch yourself spiraling down that rabbit hole of self-doubt with questions that assume the worst, hit pause. Flip the script and start asking questions that assume your power to change, grow, and find joy. It's not just about finding different answers; it's about changing the questions to reflect the incredible person you are and the amazing life you deserve. This shift doesn't just alter your expectations; it transforms your reality.

Here are 20 questions to build confidence and attract healthy relationships:

1. What unique qualities do I bring to a relationship?
2. How can I feel more self-love today?
3. What boundaries do I need to establish to feel respected and safe?
4. In what ways can I grow from my past relationship experiences?
5. How can I communicate my needs more clearly and confidently?
6. What does a healthy relationship look like to me?
7. How can I be more present and engaged in my relationships?
8. What steps can I take today to improve my emotional well-being?
9. How can I embrace vulnerability as a strength in my connections?
10. What actions can I take to nurture the relationships that matter most to me?

11. How can I let go of fears that hold me back from love?

12. What qualities do I value most in a partner, and how can I embody those myself?

13. How can I turn my past relationship challenges into learning opportunities?

14. In what ways can I show appreciation for myself and my loved ones today?

15. How can I actively create the love life I envision?

16. What can I do to make my personal happiness a priority in relationships?

17. How can practicing gratitude daily enhance my relationships?

18. What can I learn about myself through my interactions with others?

19. How can I balance giving and receiving in my relationships to foster mutual respect and affection?

20. What steps can I take to attract relationships that align with my core values and aspirations?

When we start tapping into these empowering questions, it's like flipping a switch. Instead of zeroing in on what we're missing, we get to focus on all the good stuff we can bring into our lives.

This kind of shift doesn't just boost our confidence but also paves the way for relationships that are healthier and more rewarding.

Questions steer the direction of where we are headed. Pick the ones that lift you up, and you'll see your world start to change, mirroring back all that good energy you're putting out there.

DOWNLOAD THE FREE
ENERGY VAMPIRE
DETECTION KIT

THOSE PESKY EMOTIONS

Alright, let's sit down and have a real talk about these Energy Vampires of emotions. You know, those feelings like shame, guilt, anxiety, fear — they can really suck the life out of you. But here's the thing: they're not just random feelings. They're like little messengers, telling you about what's going on in your mind.

Emotions: Your Inner Dashboard Signals

Think of your emotions as indicator lights on a car's dashboard. They light up to tell you something. If you're feeling shame or guilt, it's like your mind's way of saying, "Hey, we're thinking about something that's not making us feel too good here." These emotions signal that your thoughts are focused on something that's dragging you down, not lifting you up.

The Power of Focus

What you focus on really shapes your emotional world. It's like when you're watching a sad movie, and you feel all weepy — that's because your focus is on something sad. The same goes for when you're thinking about stuff that makes you anxious or fearful. Your focus is like a spotlight, and whatever it shines on, grows in your emotional garden.

Fear and Growth: Two Sides of the Same Coin

Fears are like big, flashing neon signs pointing to where you're ready to grow the most. It's as if they're saying, "Hey, this is your next big thing to conquer!" When you feel fear, it's not just an obstacle; it's an opportunity for some serious personal growth and learning.

Flipping the Script on Negative Emotions

So, what do you do with all these Energy Vampire emotions? First, recognize them for what they are — indicators. They're not there to mess up your day but to show you what you're focusing on. Then, start flipping the script. If you're feeling guilt, ask yourself, "What thought is causing this?" Maybe you're focusing on a mistake you made. Flip it by focusing on how you can learn from that mistake or make amends.

Embracing the Emotions

And here's the kicker — don't run from these emotions. Embrace them. Feel them. They're part of your journey. By understanding them, you can start to control where your spotlight of focus goes. Shine it on things that make you feel strong, happy, and empowered.

Fear into Action

With fear, especially, use it as a fuel. It's showing you what's important to you and what you care about. Use that energy to take action, to grow, to learn. It's like turning on the lights in a dark room — suddenly, the scary shadows aren't so scary anymore.

So, next time you feel like these Energy Vampires of emotion are visiting you, take a moment and ask yourself: "What am I focusing on?" and "How can I shift this focus to something that helps me grow?" Your emotions are powerful tools, not just obstacles. Use them to guide you to a more empowered, focused, and growth-oriented mindset. Remember, in every emotion, there's a chance to learn and a chance to shine even brighter.

Emotional Scoreboard

Now let's take these emotions onto the relationship playing field. Imagine your emotional life as a grand stadium where Team Positive and Team Negative are battling for the championship. It's the ultimate love match, where the players on the field are your feelings, and the game's outcome impacts the destiny of your relationship.

Team Positive brings its A-game with trust, communication, affection, and shared laughter, making every day feel like you're both winning the lottery of love. They're about those moments that feel like scenes from your favorite rom-com, where everything clicks, and you're both in sync, dancing through life's challenges with grace and a smile.

On the opposing side, Team Negative plays a tougher game, bringing in misunderstandings, jealousy, neglect, and conflicts. Their strategy involves turning minor issues into major dramas, making the relationship feel more like a battleground than a safe haven.

Now, imagine looking up at that giant scoreboard in your relationship. Which team is taking the lead? Are you and your partner high-fiving each other under the victorious banner of Team Positive, or are you both needing a timeout to regroup from Team Negative's advances?

The twist in this game is realizing that both you and your partner are co-referees as well as key players. You have the power to call plays, introduce new strategies, and ultimately decide which team dominates the field. Embracing open communication, patience, understanding, and forgiveness can be game-changers, shifting the momentum towards Team Positive.

If Team Negative is scoring too easily, it's time for a game plan overhaul. This could mean seeking couples' therapy, committing to regular date nights to reconnect, or simply learning to listen more deeply to each other's needs and desires.

Celebrating when Team Positive scores—acknowledging the effort it takes to make each other happy, appreciating the little things, and continuously working on strengthening your bond—keeps the love game interesting and rewarding.

So, in the grand stadium of your relationship, which team are you cheering for? How can you both ensure that Team Positive keeps the lead, making your relationship a source of joy, support, and mutual growth? Remember, every day is an opportunity to score more points for love, understanding, and happiness. Let's play this game with heart, commitment, and an eye always on the prize—a loving, fulfilling partnership.

Plot Twist in Our Relationship Game

What if, despite your best efforts, you find yourself teamed up with an Energy Vampire? This player doesn't just miss the passes but drains the very spirit of Team Positive, turning every match into a solo struggle rather than a duo's triumph.

When you're giving it your all—cheering, strategizing, playing with heart—and you still find the scoreboard tipping unfavorably, it might be time to reassess your team dynamic. It's tough when you realize that, instead of lifting each other up, one partner consistently brings the energy down, making the relationship feel more like a solo battle against the odds than a united front.

In such cases, the question isn't just about quitting the team; it's about recognizing your worth and the value you bring to the game of love. It's about understanding that sometimes, to truly win at relationships, you might need to play independently for a while. This doesn't mean you've lost; it means you're giving yourself the chance to find a teammate who matches your enthusiasm, commitment, and positive energy.

Detoxing from a relationship with an Energy Vampire means stepping off the field, catching your breath, and focusing on self-care and rebuilding your own strength. It's a time to rediscover what makes you happy, to reconnect with your passions, and to nurture your well-being, away from the draining influences.

And remember, being an independent player isn't about being alone; it's about being open to joining new teams, exploring new games, and finding someone whose spirit of play matches yours. Someone who understands that relationships are about mutual support, shared victories, and facing challenges together with courage and love.

So, if you find yourself constantly trying to score points for Team Positive while dodging the energy-sapping tactics of an uncooperative partner, consider taking a time-out. Reflect on your needs, your desires, and your worth. Remember, the goal is not just to play but to enjoy the game, to thrive, and to find a partnership that's truly a win-win.

In the grand game of love, sometimes the bravest move is to seek a new team, one that values and celebrates your strengths, where the game plan is built on mutual respect, joy, and genuine connection. Here's to finding that team where you're not just playing to win, but playing for the love of the game itself.

ENERGY VAMPIRE VIBES

R ight now is the perfect moment to shine a spotlight on the kind of energy we're inviting into our lives. Picture yourself as the DJ of your own existence, mixing and matching the tracks of your emotions and thoughts. And guess what? The universe is tuning in, bobbing its head to the rhythm of your vibe.

Your vibe—it's essentially your life's playlist. It reverberates through the nooks and crannies of your existence, syncing up with energies that match its beat. It's like trying to tune into a radio frequency. You wouldn't expect to catch a smooth jazz tune on a hard rock station. Similarly, our energy vibes with what it projects, not necessarily what we daydream about. If your current playlist is heavy on stress, doubt, or downers, you're basically sending out invites for more of the same to crash your party.

Now, let's talk about those pesky Energy Vampires and the sneaky Inner Vampire. Picture Energy Vampires as those catchy but annoying tunes that loop in your head non-stop. They linger because they resonate with something deep inside us—our Inner Vampire. This shadowy figure thrives on our fears, insecurities, and drama, scripting love stories with more twists and turns than a soap opera.

But here's the twist—you have the power to switch up your playlist from melancholy melodies to tracks filled with hope and happiness. Kickstart this transformation by showing those Energy Vampires the exit. Dial down their volume to amplify your own true voice.

This Valentine's detox is your chance to fine-tune your frequency to one that truly reflects you—the authentic, optimistic, genuinely happy you. It's about broadcasting vibes that say, "I'm all about love, positivity, and meaningful connections." And when you do, you'll start attracting the kind of people and experiences that are in harmony with your new tune. It's not just hopeful thinking; it's about aligning with the frequencies that bring in all the goodness you've been wishing for.

So, how do you remix your vibe? Begin by kindly escorting those Energy Vampires to the exit. Next, it's time for a heart-to-heart with your Inner Vampire. Recognize it, understand its motives, but don't let it steal the spotlight. Clean up the internal dialogue. Ask yourself uplifting questions. Fill your mind with thoughts and emotions that elevate you. Nourish gratitude, focus on your joys, and engage in activities that spark your inner light.

Remember, life's vibe is everything. When you vibrate with love, joy, and positivity, you turn into a magnet for the same. Your vibe really does attract your tribe, and this tribe will mirror the energy you're spreading in the world.

As Valentine's Day approaches, reflect on the energy you're emitting. Are you radiating love, self-respect, and happiness? Because that's precisely what will echo back to you. It's about crafting a vibe that's so genuinely you, so authentically yours.

When an Energy Vampire is part of your scene, it's like being cast in a role that's always off-stage, never in the spotlight. It's exhausting, dispiriting, and can turn Valentine's Day from a love story into a thriller you didn't sign up for.

But here's the good news—identifying these vampires is your cue to show them the door. It's about drawing lines, engaging in genuine conversations, and, most importantly, realizing you're worthy of a relationship that energizes you, not one that leaves you feeling drained.

So this Valentine's, let's focus less on the external tokens of affection and more on taking a real look at our relationships. Are they uplifting, or are they depleting your spirit? It's time to clear the air of Energy Vampires and welcome in the kind of love that truly nourishes. Here's to a Valentine's Detox that celebrates authenticity and self-love, stripping away the facade to rediscover the joy of being unapologetically you.

VICTIM & BLAME FATIGUE

Do you know of anyone who overplays the blame game and is a professional victim in their own story?

They're caught in a loop where every mishap in their love life is never their doing. If this sounds all too familiar, and you're tied to such a person, it's a draining experience, leading you down the path of Victim-Blame fatigue. You're worn out from all the emotional draining.

Living in this victim-blame cycle is like viewing the world through a distorted lens, where the mantra 'it's-not-my-fault' clouds your vision. You're trapped in a merry-go-round of toxic relationships, and whenever things don't pan out, pointing fingers becomes the norm. It's never about your actions or inactions. Instead, it's about your partner being too much or too little of something, or perhaps, the universe seemingly plotting against you. This mindset? It's a dead-end on the road to personal evolution.

But here's the kicker—this whole blame and victim game is emotional quicksand. Every time you point the finger or retreat into that helpless victim role, you're handing over pieces of your power. You're essentially letting others dictate your love narrative. And honestly, who desires a story where they're not steering the ship?

Let's envision a new chapter. One where you reclaim your power, transforming your narrative from being passive to taking the reins. Swap out the "Why does this always happen to me?" for a proactive "What can I learn from this?" Shift from being a passive character to the protagonist who's in charge of their destiny.

Here's the real deal: When you position yourself as the hero, every love life hiccup morphs into a chance for growth. That relationship that fizzled? It's not a testament to your lack of worth but a milestone towards realizing your true desires and necessities. Those fights and miscommunications? They're not mere conflicts but opportunities to hone your communication skills and empathy.

And the cherry on top of moving past the victim mindset? You begin to magnetize a different kind of energy. It's like retuning your personal radio station to a frequency that vibrates with strength, optimism, and self-reliance. And here's the beautiful part—this new vibe is precisely what attracts healthier, more meaningful connections.

With Valentine's Day on the horizon, what better time to kickstart this transformation? It's your personal season to cleanse from those destructive patterns and energies that have been your shackles. It's about bidding adieu to the Energy Vampires and your Inner Vampire who feast on your vulnerabilities.

As we approach a Valentine's Detox, let's consciously choose to embrace our hero role. It's our moment to take the helm of our love stories, weaving tales brimming with growth, resilience, and good energy. Remember, the most legendary love stories are those where the protagonist confronts their challenges boldly and emerges triumphant. Let this Valentine's be the prologue of your own magnificent saga.

Be Your Own Hero

Is your relationship letting you be the true hero of your own story, or does it feel more like you're stuck playing a side character in someone else's drama? Let's talk about stepping into the hero role, especially with Valentine's detox in mind. It's all about shaking off those patterns that don't serve you and embracing habits, rituals, and people who lift you up.

Imagine starting each day not just by rolling out of bed, but by setting a tone that screams, "I'm in charge here." Maybe it's stretching to your favorite tune, scribbling down what you're grateful for, or just sipping your coffee while planning how to conquer the world (or at least your to-do list). These aren't just morning routines; they're your way of saying, "Hey, I got this."

The hero life is built on habits and rituals that make you feel good inside out. Cooking up something tasty and healthy because you love treating your body right, diving into a book because learning is your jam, or jotting down three things you did well today because, well, why not celebrate the small wins?

Now, who you hang with plays a huge part in this hero gig. Surround yourself with folks who get you, who cheer for you, and who're there when the going gets tough. These are your people – the ones who make you laugh, think, and feel like you can take on anything. It's about finding your tribe and sticking with them through thick and thin.

And here's where it gets real: being the hero means sometimes you gotta make the hard calls. Maybe it's telling someone who's all take and no give that you need a break, or deciding that a situation just isn't right for you anymore. It's not being selfish; it's about making sure you're in the best place to keep being awesome.

Being the hero of your life, especially as you navigate the murky waters of Valentine's detox, is about more than just surviving; it's about thriving. It's choosing every day to live in a way that's true to you, from the moment you wake up to the people you let into your life. It's about ditching the drama, embracing growth, and, most importantly, writing your own story where you're not just a character, but the star.

So, as Valentine's Day rolls around, let's not just focus on the chocolates and the roses. Let's use it as a kickstarter to really look at our lives and relationships. Are they helping you be the hero you're meant to be? If not, maybe it's time for a little detox – a chance to reset, to focus on what really matters, and to start living like the hero you truly are.

PART 4

AUTHENTICALLY YOU

In a world of masquerades and endless charades,
where many a facade is meticulously made,
Be the rare gem, authentically true,
Embracing yourself, through and through.

Dance to the beat of your own heart's drum,
sing your soul's melody, don't succumb to the chorus
of conformity, dull and dim, shine your light,
let them see the true hymn.

Wear your quirks like a crown, oh so proud,
laugh too loud, dream too big, stand unbowed.
For in the canvas of existence, vibrant and vast,
It's the colors of authenticity that forever last.

So, twirl in your truth, in the sunlight bask,
in your genuine glow, let the world unmask.
The beauty of being real, raw, and rare,
is a treasure beyond compare, beyond compare.

Let your spirit soar, let your true self fly,
Across the boundless, azure sky.
For when you're authentically you, my friend,
you'll find the joy that knows no end.

—David Lloyd Strauss

KEYS TO AUTHENTICITY

I s your relationship playing out on a stage where you can truly be yourself, or is it a script you're following, written by someone else? Imagine living a life where every day feels like you're wearing an outfit that's just not "you." That's what it's like when your relationship doesn't align with your authentic self.

Being authentic means your dreams, desires, and even your quirks are front and center, celebrated, not just tolerated. But if you find yourself constantly adjusting your volume, dialing down your needs to avoid rocking the boat, you're not living your truth. It's perfectly natural to crave a partnership where understanding, support, and laughter are abundant.

So, what happens when your relationship feels more constraining than empowering? It's not about pointing fingers or placing blame but recognizing when the fit isn't right. Maybe it's time to ask yourself if you're compromising too much of who you are in the name of love.

Choosing authenticity isn't the easy route. It might mean making difficult decisions, facing uncomfortable truths, and potentially starting anew. But the reward? A life where you're free to be you, surrounded by love that celebrates, not just accommodates, your true self. Because, in the end, being authentically you is the ultimate journey towards fulfillment and happiness.

Being authentically you, embracing your true self, paves the way to a life where you can freely explore and fulfill the seven essential keys of authenticity.

The 7 Keys

1 - Connection & Belonging

We're all looking for that warm fuzzy feeling, right? Whether it's with family, friends, or that special someone, feeling connected and loved is like the ultimate human craving. Everyone needs to feel a part of something, to connect deeply with others, whether that's through love, friendship, or shared causes. It's about feeling welcomed, understood, and valued by those around us.

2 - Spontaneity & Change

This need spices up life with excitement and new experiences. It's the drive for unexpected pleasures, surprises, and the thrill of the unknown—keeping us vibrant and engaged. Life without surprises would be like eating the same meal every day. Boring, right? We need changes, challenges, and a bit of spice to keep things interesting.

3 - Recognition & Importance

This need taps into our desire to feel acknowledged and significant. It's about knowing that we matter, that our contributions are valued and that we have impacted the world or our personal circles. Deep down, we all want to feel like we matter, like we're making a mark on the world in our own unique way. It's about feeling valued and important.

4 - Stability & Security

While we crave adventure, we also need a solid foundation. This need is about having a predictable environment where we feel safe, secure, and comfortable, providing a balance to our desire for variety. Knowing there's some predictability in our lives gives us peace of mind.

5 - Evolution & Advancement

Growth is about moving forward, learning, and expanding our horizons. It's the pursuit of personal development, acquiring new skills, and deepening our understanding of ourselves and the world. If we're not growing and advancing, we're just standing still, and who wants that? Personal development and learning new things keep life exciting.

6 - Generosity & Impact

This is the need to give back, to contribute to the well-being of others, and to leave a positive mark on the world. It's about leaving a legacy and feeling part of something bigger.

7 - Authenticity & Self-Expression

The need to be our true selves and to express our thoughts, feelings, and beliefs openly and honestly. It's about living in alignment with our values and sharing our unique perspective with the world.

When you're in a relationship that supports the seven keys, it feels like everything clicks into place. You're free to express love and feel deeply connected, not just on special occasions but in the quiet moments too.

There's a thrilling mix of stability and surprises, keeping you both engaged and excited about the future together. You feel valued for who you are, not just for what you do, which boosts your sense of significance.

There's a comforting certainty in knowing you have a solid foundation, yet enough flexibility for personal growth and shared adventures. Together, you contribute to each other's lives and the world around you in meaningful ways, creating a legacy of love and support.

On the flip side, if these pillars aren't present in your relationship, it can feel like you're constantly reaching for something that's just out of grasp. The lack of connection leaves you feeling isolated, even when you're together.

Without spontaneity, life starts to feel monotonous, like you're both just going through the motions.

If your need for importance is unmet, you might find yourself questioning your value in the relationship.

An absence of stability and security can create anxiety about the future, making it hard to plan or dream together.

Stunted growth, a lack of evolution and advancement leaves you feeling stagnant, as if you're not moving forward.

And without generosity and impact, it's challenging to feel like you're part of something greater, reducing the joy and fulfillment that comes from giving back.

When these seven keys aren't part of your relationship, it's tough to feel authentically you, and the relationship with suffer.

SANDBOX DREAMS

L et's double down on something important here, especially when we're talking about shaking off those not-so-great relationship vibes. It's about the stories we tell ourselves—that internal script that's been running in our heads since day one.

Every one of us has a story about our life that has shaped who we are, how we see ourselves, and even the kind of love we think we deserve. It's like our own personal storybook, with its own heroes, villains, triumphs, and heartaches. And here's the rub: these stories are powerful. They shape our self-image, influence our decisions, and color our relationships.

But where do these stories come from? They start from those tiny seeds of early childhood, watered by the people around us—our family, friends, teachers, all those childhood experiences, and the environment we grow up in. Every relationship and every encounter throughout our lives adds another layer to our story.

Think about it this way: our childhood is like this wild, beautiful garden, and in this garden, you have two types of people: Dream Weavers and Dream Stealers.

Dream Weavers? They're like sunshine and rain, helping us grow tall and strong. They sprinkle all this positivity and confidence on us. They're the cheerleaders in our life, always there to boost us up, celebrate our victories—big and small—and make us believe we can conquer the world.

But not everyone's garden gets that sunny treatment. Enter the Dream Stealers. These are like a never-ending eclipse over our garden. They bring in clouds of doubt, fear, and negativity. They could be anyone — parents who were a bit too tough, friends who weren't really friends, anyone who made our self-esteem take a hit. And guess what? This negativity sticks with us as we grow up. It shapes how we see love, treat ourselves, and even our choices in our relationships. It's like these early experiences set the stage for our future love stories — whether they're epic romances or a bit of a rollercoaster.

When we were kids, our imaginations were like this endless sky of fireworks — colorful, wild, and bursting with dreams. Remember those days in the park, playing with toys and dolls? We called them our 'sandbox dreams.' In that sandbox, anything was possible. Astronaut, superhero, wizard — you name it, we could become it. Our imaginations had no limits, no fences. They were as free as birds in the sky.

But here's the thing — as we grow up, life throws curveballs. Challenges, fears, and insecurities start creeping in like shadows, dimming the brightness of our childhood dreams. It's like watching the colors in our garden fade away. Those once vibrant dreams start to get tangled up in the 'what ifs' and 'I can'ts.' It's a bittersweet goodbye to our creativity.

Our imaginations, once our superpowers, can start playing tricks on us. Thanks to the influence of Dream Weavers and Dream Stealers, our imagination becomes this double-edged sword. Do we use it to keep building castles in the air, to keep dreaming big? Or do we let it take a backseat, clouded by doubts and fears?

Picture this: You're standing at the crossroads of then and now. On one side, there's that wide-eyed, sandbox-loving kid with dreams bigger than the sky. On the other, you're the adult, navigating a world that's a bit more complex, a bit more real. But who says you can't keep a bit of that childhood magic in your back pocket? Let's keep those dreams vivid and alive, coloring our world with the shades of hope and joy, not fear or regret.

Then boom, along comes Valentine's Day. It's that moment when you take a good, hard look at your love life and ask, "Is this the epic tale of romance I imagined?" It's more than just roses and chocolates; it's a reality check. A chance to see how our own stories, those inner dialogues of doubt and fear, are playing out in our relationship.

But here's the twist in our plot: we're the heroes of our own story. We've got the power to flip the script. To move from tales of self-doubt to sagas of self-love. It's like gardening for the soul; we're uprooting those weeds of negativity and planting fresh seeds of confidence and self-worth.

So, let's reinvigorate our childlike imagination, take that pen, turn the page, and start writing a love story that makes our hearts sing. After all, we're crafting our own fairytales here, and it's about time they had a happy ending, right?

UNRAVELING TOXIC TIES

Have you ever wondered why you're stuck in a relationship that feels more like a merry-go-round than a forward-moving journey? It's as if the same issues, arguments, and disappointments keep popping up, yet this invisible force keeps you from pressing the eject button. With Valentine's Day casting its glow (or shadow, depending on where you stand), it is the perfect time to step back, grab a metaphorical flashlight, and illuminate the thought patterns that have you circling these toxic tracks.

Setting the Scene with What You Allow

Dive into this gem of wisdom: "What you allow, you teach." When we let certain behaviors slide in our relationships, it's akin to drafting a rulebook that says, "This is okay with me." Picture rolling out a red carpet for disrespect or indifference to make its grand entrance. If your partner keeps flaking on plans and you respond with silence, you're essentially signing off on this behavior as acceptable. By dismissing hurtful comments or justifying poor behavior, you're engraving these patterns into the foundation of your relationship, signaling a thumbs-up to this treatment.

Green-lighting the Bad Stuff

The way we permit others to treat us is like signaling them with a green light. It's an unspoken agreement defined by our reactions—or sometimes, our lack of them. Each time we brush off actions that genuinely bother us, it's as if we're saying, "Sure, continue, I'm fine with it." But are we really?

Self-Worth: The Story Behind the Scenes

More often than not, this cycle can be traced back to our personal narrative about self-worth. If we're harboring beliefs deep down that we don't deserve better, we naturally end up in situations that reflect this low valuation of ourselves. It's as though we're viewing our relationships through a lens smeared with our doubts about our worth, obscuring the vision of what we truly deserve.

Fear: The Invisible Shackles

Fear is a cunning architect of barriers that keep us tethered to less-than-ideal situations. The apprehension about ending up alone, the anxiety of not finding someone else, or the trepidation of facing conflict—these fears construct walls around us, making the idea of leaving a toxic relationship seem more daunting than staying.

Embracing Courage for Change

So, here's a thought: why not take this Valentine's as an opportunity for a heart-to-heart with yourself? It's time to recognize the toxic loops and realize we hold the remote to change the channel. It's an invitation to reassess, to rediscover our self-worth, and to confront our fears with a fresh dose of courage.

Deepening the Dive: Further Steps to Break Free

Awareness is your lantern in the dark: Start noticing your thoughts and reactions. Be mindful when you're rationalizing behaviors that don't align with your well-being. Confront your fears: What truly is the worst that could happen if you assert yourself or walk away? More often than not, the reality is less frightening than the fear itself.

Level Up Your Self-worth

Engage in practices that boost how you feel about yourself. This could be through affirmations, therapy, or simply by choosing to spend time with those who uplift you. Establish clear boundaries: Communicate what you're comfortable with and what's off-limits. Boundaries are the backbone of any healthy relationship.

Seek Support

Seeking support is like calling in the cavalry when you're feeling a bit cornered in your own love story. Sometimes, you're so deep in the forest you can't see the trees – or, in relationship terms, you're too caught up in the emotional whirlwind to spot the exit sign. That's where your squad comes in, be it your friends, a therapist, or a bunch of strangers who've been in the same boat and lived to tell the tale.

Chatting with friends is like opening up your personal think tank. They know you, love you, and most importantly, they're not afraid to tell you when you're veering off course. They're the ones who'll hand you a flashlight when you're stumbling in the dark, helping you navigate through the mess. Plus, a good venting session can be as refreshing as a weekend getaway.

Now, therapists – they're like your personal emotional navigators. With a map of the human psyche in hand, they guide you through the choppy waters of your feelings, helping you understand why you're sailing in circles. It's a bit like having a GPS for your emotions; suddenly, the route to "Better Place" starts looking a lot clearer.

And support groups? Picture this: a roundtable of fellow voyagers, each with their own battle scars and stories of survival. It's a reminder that you're not alone on this journey. Sharing your story and hearing others can be incredibly grounding. It's like discovering a hidden playlist of empowerment anthems – suddenly, you're part of a chorus singing "We Will Survive."

No matter which route you choose, reaching out is about adding extra oars to your lifeboat. It's about broadening your perspective, gaining clarity, and sometimes, just finding the strength to paddle one more day. So, go ahead, send out that signal flare, and watch as the support pours in. Remember, even the mightiest ships sometimes need a lighthouse to guide them home.

Self-care

Self-care during a Valentine's detox – it's not just about bubble baths and face masks, though those are pretty great, too. It's about taking care of your whole self: body, mind, emotions, spirit, and your social world. Let's break it down, shall we?

Body: It's time to treat your body like the temple it is, especially when you're detoxing from a relationship that left you feeling less than stellar. This means feeding yourself nutritious foods that make you feel energized, not sluggish. Get moving – dance around your living room, take a yoga class, go for a run. It's all about releasing those endorphins and reminding yourself of the strength you carry in your bones.

Mind: Your brain's probably been on a bit of a rollercoaster, huh? Give it a break. Dive into a good book, meditate, or simply spend some time each day in quiet reflection. The goal is to clear the mental clutter and focus on thoughts that serve you, empower you, and move you forward.

Emotions: This is a biggie. Allowing yourself to feel what you're feeling without judgment is key. Sadness, anger, relief – it's all valid. Writing in a journal or expressing yourself through art can be incredibly therapeutic. It's about acknowledging your emotions but not letting them hold the steering wheel.

Spiritual: Whatever spirituality means to you, now's the time to connect with it. For some, it might mean prayer or attending religious services. For others, it could be nature walks, meditation, or spending time on personal development. This connection can provide a sense of peace and purpose that's especially welcome during times of change.

Social: Surround yourself with people who lift you up, who make you laugh, who remind you that you're not alone in this world. This might mean leaning on close friends and family or joining new groups that share your interests. It's about creating a community that supports you, just as you are.

Valentine's detox isn't just about stepping away from a toxic relationship; it's about stepping into a more holistic approach to self-care. It's recognizing that you're a beautifully complex being deserving of care in all aspects of your life. So, as you navigate this season, remember to nurture your body, soothe your mind, honor your emotions, deepen your spiritual connections, and cherish your social circles. This holistic self-care is your path to healing, growth, and ultimately, to finding a love that starts with you.

WHEN IS ENOUGH ENOUGH?

Have you ever had one of those look-back moments? It's like when you realize you've been on a rollercoaster way too long that's been spinning in circles. You've had your fill of the dizzying highs and lows, and now you're ready to step off and find some solid ground. Figuring out when to say 'enough' is a major turning point.

Think about it. Being in a toxic relationship is like being in a boat that's constantly rocking. Sometimes, it's the big waves of drama crashing over you, other times, it's those subtle ripples of unease. But the boat's only rocky because you're in there with an Energy Vampire.

They're the ones stirring up the waters with their Taker tendencies, Drama Queen antics, or Blamer habits. You've tried bailing out the water, patching up the holes, but the boat keeps rocking.

Then, there's this moment. It's quiet, introspective, almost like the eye of the storm. You start thinking, "Is this it? Is this what love is supposed to feel like?" You remember those dreams you had, the ones where love was a two-way street, filled with mutual respect, support, and genuine care. Not this endless game of emotional tug-of-war.

It's in this moment of clarity you realize that your self-worth has been buried under layers of doubt, criticism, and neglect. You've been so focused on trying to fix things, to fill the voids in your partner, that you've forgotten to take care of yourself. It's like you've been feeding your self-esteem to an invisible monster that's never satisfied.

So, you start thinking about walking away. Not because you don't care, but because you care about yourself too. It's not giving up; it's stepping up — for your own well-being. It's acknowledging that this toxic dance you've been in is not the tango of love but a limbo of diminishing self-respect.

Walking away, though, isn't just about physically leaving. It's an emotional and mental journey. It's about rebuilding those parts of you that got lost in the relationship. It's about rediscovering your passions, your dreams, and the simple joys that make you, well, you.

And here's where the magic starts happening. As you step away from the toxicity, you begin to see yourself in a new light. You realize that you're stronger than you gave yourself credit for. You start to rebuild your self-confidence, not from external validation, but from an inner sense of self-worth.

You find new hobbies, new friends, and new environments that resonate with who you truly are. It's like planting a garden in a place that was once barren. You nurture it, watch it grow, and soon, you've got this beautiful space that's all yours — a reflection of your true self.

How do you know when is enough, actually enough? It's like hitting that snooze button one too many times on a Monday morning — at some point, you've just got to get up.

Let's dive into the four stages of relationship detox that will help you figure out where you stand in the heart of your relationship. These stages are like signposts on your journey, pointing out if you're on a path that feels right or if you've veered off into the thick of things.

From that first nudge of realization to the moment you decide it's time to lace up your boots and walk towards something new, each stage is a stepping stone towards understanding what "enough" means to you. Let's stroll through these stages together, uncovering what it really looks like to choose paths that lead us to where we genuinely want to be.

FOUR STAGES OF
LOVE DETOX

Awakening to Reality: The Eye-Opener

Imagine you've been sailing on autopilot, enjoying the breeze, but missing out on the scenery. This first stage is like the moment you decide to really look around, and suddenly, you see the leaks in your boat. It's a gentle wake-up call, urging you to pay attention to the parts of your relationship you've been glossing over. Maybe it's patterns you've ignored or excuses you've made for things that weren't quite right. It's about acknowledging that, hey, there's more to this love story than meets the eye. It's not about blame or regret; it's about realizing there's room for improvement for both you and your relationship.

Seeing the Light: The Clarity Phase

Now, with your eyes wide open, you start to see things in HD. This stage is all about clarity—recognizing the not-so-great parts of your relationship and understanding how they've affected you. It's like you've been trying to complete a puzzle with missing pieces, and suddenly, you find them under the sofa. It might be uncomfortable, realizing you've been missing these pieces all along, but it's also empowering. You're now equipped with the knowledge of what's been holding you back, and with knowledge comes power—the power to change, to grow, and to move towards healthier, happier relationship dynamics.

Questioning the Path —The Crossroads

Here's where things get real. You're standing at a crossroads, with paths stretching out in every direction. This stage is about questioning everything—the good, the bad, and the ugly. It's about looking at your relationship and asking, "Is this really what I want? Does this path lead me to the version of myself I aspire to be?" It's decision time, and while that might feel daunting, it's also incredibly freeing. You're no longer a passenger; you're the captain of your ship, deciding where to set sail. This stage is a mix of introspection, courage, and a dash of boldness, as you choose the path that aligns with your deepest desires and values.

Conscious Departure — The New Journey

Making the choice to leave a relationship that no longer serves you is both an ending and a beginning. This stage is about moving forward, but with intention and purpose. It's not a rash escape but a thoughtful journey towards a life that feels more authentic and fulfilling. You're armed with lessons learned and insights gained, ready to embark on a new adventure—one that's more in tune with who you are and who you want to be. This stage is about embracing your newfound independence, exploring new horizons, and opening your heart to the possibilities that await. It's a celebration of growth, resilience, and the exciting unknown.

Throughout these four stages, remember: this detox isn't just about shedding the old; it's about making space for the new. It's a journey of self-discovery, self-love, and, ultimately, self-empowerment. So, as you navigate through each phase, keep your eyes on the horizon and your heart open to change. This Valentine's season, let's toast to new beginnings and to being authentically, unapologetically you.

STOP WINDOW SHOPPING FOR HAPPINESS!

Have you ever found yourself peering through the glass window of life, window shopping for happiness as if it were a gift out of your reach that you can never receive?

Here's a gentle nudge: Your life is that gift you've been looking for, sitting right in your lap. It's your own epic adventure, and guess what? You're leading the charge. With Valentine's Detox in the air, it's the perfect moment to grab the pen and start scripting your love story. If you're not steering, you might end up living a tale someone else has jotted down. And honestly, who's down for that?

Window shopping for happiness is all about getting real. It's peeling back those layers to see what's actually happening in your world. How's your heart doing? Are you walking the path you've dreamt of? Being straight with yourself is crucial—it's like unlocking your own handcuffs. And once you see your life for what it is, that's when you find this incredible power within. You start to shake off the chains of past haunts and move forward.

That clarity, it's got some serious mojo. Being honest about where you stand, especially in love, is like opening the door to a whole new chapter. Suddenly, every little stumble is a chance to grow. Think of it as realizing that every hiccup on the road is actually a step up to becoming your best self.

Reflecting on the ups and downs, those moments that feel less than great? They're actually nudges pushing you to face the music. Life's tossing you a choice: let the waves carry you or grab the helm and sail. Choosing to own your feelings and decisions? That's like hopping from the passenger seat to taking the wheel.

Blaming others for the dips in our love lives is the path of least resistance, but it's like jogging in place—you don't really get anywhere. Stepping up and owning every bit of your love life, that's like unlocking a new level of freedom. It's a farewell to those draining relationship vibes and a big hello to a journey filled with growth, resilience, and genuine joy.

Our inner doubts, those negative whispers? We all have them. But here's the kicker: the moment we're capable of thinking for ourselves, we get to set the course. Our thoughts, feelings, actions? We call the shots. No one gets a say in how we feel without our say-so. It's about taking the reins of our love narrative.

We've all had those love experiences that didn't quite hit the mark. Maybe we pointed fingers, blaming circumstances or others. Yet, when the curtain falls, it's on us to interpret and react to these moments. We have the power to star as the hero or play the victim.

Heroes in love? They're the ones hunting for solutions, owning their stories, and stepping into action. Victims remain stuck, dwelling on what was. But here's the deal: choosing to be the hero is just that—a choice.

If your love story isn't shaping up how you'd like, it's time to make a move. Boost your self-love, take control, and initiate changes. Remember, you're crafting your own narrative, not just a bystander.

So, this Valentine's Detox, let's stop the window shopping for happiness. It's about recognizing where you're at, embracing your worth, and tackling those fears head-on. It's your story, your terms. Set a new standard for love and life. Draw that line, step into your future, and own every part of your journey. You're the architect of your experiences, the author of your joy. Dive into life's driver's seat. Everything you're living right now? It's your creation, and yes, you can alter the blueprint. Start by making a choice, followed by bold, decisive action. Clear the clutter, embrace the new, and no more excuses.

Let go of the past, don't glance back, and fully own every slice of your life. Happiness, health, love—it's on you to pivot your mindset and take fresh steps. Tune out those doubting voices. Instead, listen to your heart, your intuition. Take charge of your destiny. How you see yourself is key. Not feeling it? Change the vibe. Free yourself from yesterday's shadows and step into your dreams with courage.

Decide today: your life, your rules. Trust in yourself. Embrace every moment as a lesson in growth. It's your life, your love story. And you've got all the power to pen it precisely how you've always wanted.

YOUR PERSONAL
DREAM TEAM

So, you've finally stepped out of that toxic loop, and suddenly, there's this whole new space opening up in front of you. It's like, "Okay, what now?" It's the perfect time to start thinking about who you want in your corner as you step into this fresh chapter of your life. Picture this as your moment to draft your very own dream team as you dive into the whole Valentine's Detox vibe.

Gathering Your Crew

Think about it like picking your squad for the ultimate road trip. You want folks who bring out the best in you, who make the journey fun, and who can navigate the map when you hit a dead end. These are the new faces, the fresh vibes you're inviting into your life. They're the kind of people who not only get you but also cheer you on towards becoming the best version of yourself.

Finding the Right Fit

It's all about vibing on the same frequency. You're on the lookout for people who mirror the positive changes you're making. Maybe it's a new friend you click with over coffee, a mentor you stumble upon at a seminar, or someone special who shares your love for the great outdoors. The key? Keeping your heart and mind open to these connections.

Being a Sponge

One of the coolest things about this time in your life? You're like a sponge, ready to soak up all the wisdom around you. Drop any "I've got it all figured out" act and embrace the beauty of learning from others. This openness not only draws the right kind of folks into your life but also propels your growth in unexpected ways.

Mutual Vibes

Remember, building your dream team isn't a one-way street. It's about the give and take. Genuine connections thrive on mutual support, respect, and the happiness that comes from seeing each other succeed.

The Ripple Effect

Surrounding yourself with positive, go-getter types does wonders. Their energy, outlook, and support start to rub off on you. Suddenly, you're seeing the world in brighter colors, and you've got this squad cheering you on, believing in you even on your off days.

So, as you're stepping into this new phase, really think about who you want by your side. Your dream team isn't just there for the sunny days; they're your ride-or-die crew for when things get stormy too, ready with a laugh, a piece of advice, or just a listening ear.

Here's to building those bonds that light up your life and inspire you to chase after the best version of you. Let's make this chapter one for the books, with a team that's as dreamy as it gets.

THE GRATITUDE LENS

Gratitude is a secret superpower we all have but forget to use. Melody Beattie nailed it when she said, "Gratitude unlocks the fullness of life." It's like gratitude turns everything up a notch, from blah to fantastic.

Think about it this way: living with gratitude is like wearing heart-shaped glasses. Everything looks a bit warmer, a bit brighter. It's not just about saying "thanks" for the big stuff; it's about really feeling it, for everything, big and small. Grateful people have this knack for pulling in more good vibes into their lives, no matter how much or little they have.

And here's the best part: gratitude is like an emotional fountain of youth. It brings you peace, a clear mind, and that warm, fuzzy feeling of happiness. It's about seeing the silver lining, even when things are a bit cloudy. Gratitude takes any old thought or experience and turns it into something beautiful. It's all about that choice to be grateful.

When you're living in a state of gratitude, it's obvious. Your eyes sparkle a bit more, your heart feels lighter, and your smile, well, it's just more genuine.

Here's something interesting: when you really focus on gratitude, it's like turning up the volume on all the good stuff in your thoughts. It makes your positive vibes stronger and helps you attract the things you want faster.

Now, a lack of gratitude, that's a real Energy Vampire. It stops all the good stuff from flowing your way. It's like putting up a big "No Thanks" sign in your life.

But remember, gratitude isn't just something that happens after good stuff comes your way. It's the cause, not the effect. Feeling grateful, like you already have what you want, that's what brings the good stuff into your life. It's like ordering your favorite dish at a restaurant and knowing it's going to be amazing.

And here's the big thing about gratitude: it shows maturity. It means understanding that every challenge is really a chance to learn and grow. Living in gratitude means seeing every moment as an opportunity to plant some positive thoughts and watch them bloom.

So, as we're all trying to shake off the Valentine's blues and step away from those draining relationships, let's not forget about gratitude. It's more than just a feel-good thing; it's a way of life that can really turn things around.

Remember, your most powerful moments are the ones filled with gratitude. It's about starting and ending each day with a thankful heart and knowing that everything takes time to unfold. Gratitude isn't just a quick fix; it's a long game, and it's totally worth it.

FORGIVENESS TRAIL...

Valentine's Day can bring a whirlwind of emotions, especially for those in the midst of a love detox. It's a time when the heart's desires and disappointments are felt more acutely. In this journey, one of the most liberating steps you can take is to embrace the art of moving forward — and that often starts with forgiveness.

Forgiveness is like a breath of fresh air in a stale room. It's not about forgetting or condoning the past but about allowing yourself to step out of a cycle that no longer serves you. It's about saying, "Okay, that chapter of my life happened, but it's not going to write my future."

As you cruise through the tricky waters of past relationships, remember that holding onto resentment or regret is like carrying a backpack full of rocks — it only weighs you down. Forgiveness lightens that load. It's about looking at your past with a kind eye, understanding that every experience, no matter how painful, had its role in shaping you.

Imagine standing at a crossroads. One path is well-trodden, marked by the footprints of past grievances and hurts. The other path is less defined, a little wilder, perhaps, but it's forward-moving. This path represents forgiveness, and it's the one that leads to growth and new possibilities in love.

Forgiving is not just about others; it's also about forgiving yourself. Maybe you stayed too long in a relationship that wasn't right, or you ignored red flags. It's okay. Forgive yourself for the choices you made when you were learning and growing. Self-forgiveness is a powerful step toward self-love, which is the cornerstone of any fulfilling relationship.

As you reflect on your love life this Valentine's season, consider the role of forgiveness. It might just be the key to unlocking a happier, healthier you. Remember, every step forward is a step towards a love that respects, cherishes, and uplifts you.

THE REAL REFLECTION

When it comes to Valentine's Day and the whole detox vibe, have you ever thought about how much your self-image plays a part? It's like, the way we see ourselves is the key to pretty much everything — how we act, who we hang with, even the kind of love we attract.

Most of us are going through life with this self-image we picked up as kids, and it works until it doesn't. Especially after something big shakes up our world — like the end of a relationship. That's when you're forced to hit pause and really look at who you are. It's like the universe is giving you this blank canvas and saying, "Hey, time to paint a new picture of yourself."

And this isn't just about slapping on a fresh coat of paint. We're talking deep, introspective work here. It's about digging into your dreams, values, and even those bits you might not be super proud of. It's rediscovering the things that light you up — old hobbies, new passions, whatever makes your heart sing.

Now, let's chat about energy vampires for a sec. These characters are often a reflection of how we see ourselves. If your self-image is like, "I'm not worthy of amazing love," guess who you will attract? Yep, those energy-sucking types who reinforce that belief.

But you can totally change your self-image. Start by flipping those "I am" statements from negative to positive. Instead of telling yourself you're unworthy or unlovable, start seeing yourself as deserving of all the good stuff, especially love. This isn't just feel-good talk. It's about transforming from the inside out.

This whole self-image thing really kicks off early in life, mostly in those first five years. That's when you're like a sponge, soaking up everything around you. Those years can set you up with a killer self-image or plant the seeds for those pesky Inner Vampires. But no matter what got planted back then, you've got the power to weed it out and plant something way better.

So, this Valentine's detox is the perfect time to take a good, hard look at your self-image. Are you seeing yourself as someone who deserves awesome, healthy love? Or are you settling for less because you think that's all you're worth?

When you start changing how you see yourself, everything else starts shifting too. You'll start drawing in the kind of love that feels good, the kind that lifts you up instead of pulling you down.

In the end, it's all about stepping into this new, empowered version of yourself. It's about breaking free from the old stories and creating a love life that's as amazing as you are. So go ahead, give your self-image a makeover this Valentine's season, and watch how everything, especially love, starts falling into place.

FROM STORMS TO SANCTUARY

L et's shine light on what it's like after you step out of the storm of a toxic relationship and start healing. It's like chilling on the beach after you've been through a wild storm, looking out at this huge ocean of possibilities. It's not just a break in your life; it's a whole new chapter. Think of it as your own renaissance, where you rediscover who you really are.

This time is all about stepping into your inner sanctuary and finding yourself again. It's like getting a blank canvas after you've been working on the same old painting for years. Now, you've got the freedom to create something new that's really you. You're diving deep into who you are, figuring out what you want, what to dream about, and what really matters to you.

It's also a great time to return to things that make you happy. Maybe you've put aside a hobby you loved, or maybe there's something new you've always wanted to try. This is your chance to explore and experience life in new ways, maybe ways you've never thought of before.

Every little step you take is a step towards returning your independence and sense of self. It's all about learning to love and accept yourself for who you are. Embrace this time to really fall in love with yourself and appreciate your strength, resilience, and all the things that make you unique.

During this time, you might have moments of doubt or fear, and that's totally normal. Just remember, you're exploring new territory. But every challenge is a chance to grow stronger and more confident in who you are and what you can achieve.

This post-toxic relationship phase isn't just about healing from what's happened; it's about building a future that's full of hope and happiness. It's a journey where you'll find out that the most important relationship you'll ever have is the one with yourself. So, take a deep breath, embrace this chance for rediscovery, and start painting your new future with bright, bold colors of self-love and empowerment.

Now, let's talk about taking stock of your life. It's like you're the main character in your own story, and you're looking at everything around you. First up, the people in your life - are they lifting you up or bringing you down? Think of your relationships like a garden - which ones need some love and care, and which ones need to be weeded out?

Then, there are your daily habits. What are they saying about you? Are they helping you become the person you want to be? This isn't about being hard on yourself. It's about making sure your actions line up with your goals. Are you feeding your passions, or have they been put on the back burner? This life audit is all about focusing on what's really important to you and letting go of what's not.

Next, let's find those energy drains. They're like little leaks that are slowly draining your energy away. It could be anything — a one-sided friendship, a job that's not right for you. It's time to tackle these issues head-on. Start setting boundaries, saying 'no' more often, and making choices that protect your energy.

Don't forget about the internal energy drains, too, like that little voice in your head that's always criticizing you. It's time to be kinder to yourself. Swap out that inner critic for a cheerleader. Plug those leaks and watch your energy stay right where it should be — with you.

And now for the fun part — adding joy to your life! It's like putting splashes of color everywhere. Rediscover old hobbies or start new adventures. Create moments of joy throughout your day, whether big or small. Connect with people who make you laugh, find groups that share your interests, or help out with causes you care about. Remember, it's often the little things that bring the most happiness.

Physical self-care is super important too. Think of your body as a temple. How are you going to take care of it today? Get plenty of sleep, eat food that makes you feel great, and find ways to move that you actually enjoy. And relax! A massage, a hot bath, some yoga - whatever helps you unwind.

Now, let's not forget about your emotional and mental health. It's all about tuning in to how you're feeling. Express yourself creatively, talk to someone who really gets you, or sit with your feelings for a bit. Feed your mind with things that challenge and relax you. And when those negative thoughts start creeping in, acknowledge them and then steer them towards something more positive.

In this life journey, it's not just about embracing the present but also about painting a picture of who you aspire to be. Imagine yourself not as you are with your perceived flaws and limitations but as the very best version of yourself. This isn't a flight of fancy; it's a powerful exercise in visualization, where you feed the potential you hold within.

Let your imagination be a sanctuary where the ideal version of you lives and thrives — confident, accomplished, and radiant. As you visualize, you are not escaping reality but nurturing and empowering the seeds of your potential. This daily practice of envisioning your best self gradually transforms your reality as the qualities you imagine begin to manifest in your everyday life. Embrace this powerful tool and watch as you evolve into the person you've always dreamed of being.

Lastly, showing up for yourself every day is your secret weapon. It's your way of saying to the world, "Hey, I matter." It's not just about feeling good; it's about being the best you can be. Embrace this journey of self-care as a part of your daily life. It's not negotiable; it's essential.

By caring for yourself, you're unlocking your true potential and allowing yourself to shine in every part of your life. Embrace it and watch as your world transforms into a place that's filled with more joy, peace, and fulfillment.

WHO DO YOU WANT TO BECOME?

Starting anew can feel like standing at the edge of a vast, unexplored forest. It's daunting, sure, but it's also thrilling. You're at this incredible point where you get to ask yourself, "Who do I want to become?" It's like you've been given a blank canvas, and now, you get to paint the picture of the best version of yourself.

Imagine this: the best version of you. What does that look like? Maybe it's someone brimming with confidence, not just the superficial kind, but the deep-seated confidence that comes from truly knowing and loving yourself. It's the version of you that wakes up excited for the day, lives passionately, and doesn't shy away from challenges. It's you, being kind, not just to others, but to yourself too. It's you embracing your quirks, strengths, and weaknesses and using them all to propel yourself forward.

But to become this authentic version of yourself, you've got to let go of some heavy baggage — social constructs and societal expectations. It's like you've been carrying around a backpack filled with stones labeled 'how you should look,' 'what you should achieve by a certain age,' 'how you should behave in a relationship,' and so on. It's time to unpack that bag.

Letting go of these societal expectations means no longer measuring your worth by someone else's ruler. It's about not letting age-old narratives dictate who you should be. It's shaking off the pressure to conform to certain relationship norms, career paths, and lifestyles. It means not letting social media, with its curated, picture-perfect lives, set unrealistic standards for your happiness and success.

Most importantly, this new beginning is about redefining happiness on your terms. It's about finding joy in what truly matters to you, not what society says should make you happy. Maybe happiness for you is about exploring new hobbies, traveling, or simply enjoying a quiet life surrounded by a few close friends. Perhaps it's about pursuing a career that fulfills you, not one that looks good on paper.

In this new chapter, you're the author, and you have the freedom to craft your story as you see fit. You're not just surviving; you're thriving, blossoming into the person you were always meant to be. This journey isn't just about walking away from what doesn't serve you; it's about walking towards a life that feels genuinely yours. And in this journey, the most exciting part is discovering that the person you become is more incredible than you ever imagined.

Let's dive into some questions to help you figure out who you want to become. Imagine grabbing a cup of your favorite drink, sitting down with a journal, and really giving your undivided attention to these questions. It's all about carving out the best version of you. And don't forget, this is your journey, so feel free to tweak these questions to suit your unique path.

Life Expanding Questions
Physical Health

"How do I want to feel in my body every day?"

"What kind of physical activities do I enjoy, and how can I incorporate them into my daily routine?"

Mental Power

"What new skills or knowledge do I want to acquire?"

"How can I challenge my brain in exciting and fulfilling ways?"

Social Status

"What qualities do I value in my friendships and relationships?"

"How can I be the kind of friend/partner I wish to have?"

Emotional Flow

"What does emotional well-being mean to me?"

"How can I nurture my emotional health on a daily basis?"

Spiritual Fluidity

"What practices or beliefs deeply resonate with me?"

"How can I make my spiritual health a priority?"

Financial Aims

"What are my financial goals, and what steps am I taking to achieve them?"

"How can I manage my finances to reflect my values and priorities?"

Community Connection

"What role do I want to play in my community?"

"How can I contribute to making my community a better place?"

Contribution and Good Will

"In what ways do I want to give back or make a difference?"

"What causes are close to my heart, and how can I support them?"

Boost Your Journey

Journaling

It's like having a conversation with yourself. It helps you track your progress, understand your emotions, and clarify your thoughts. Plus, it's a priceless mirror to look into as your life progress to reflect on your life's journey. "Remember when…"

Meditation

Even just a few minutes a day can increase your self-awareness, reduce stress, and improve concentration.

Drinking Water

Sounds simple, but staying hydrated is crucial for physical and mental health.

Daily MUSTS

These are the things you commit to doing every day, no matter what. They keep you grounded and focused on your goals, whether it's a morning walk, reading, or calling a loved one.

Remember, these questions and practices are just starting points. Customize them to fit your life and your dreams. The important part is to be honest with yourself and enjoy the journey of becoming the best version of you.

Alright, let's chat about what a healthy relationship with yourself looks like and feels like on a daily basis. It's like having a best friend inside you, someone who's always rooting for you, understands you, and is there through thick and thin.

Morning Check-ins

Picture starting each day with a little self-meeting. How are you feeling today? What do you need? It's like having a morning coffee with your inner self.

Self-Talk

Imagine your inner voice as your personal cheerleader. It's kind, encouraging, and always on your side. Instead of being critical, it's more like, "Hey, you got this!" or "It's okay, let's try again."

Mindfulness

Throughout the day, it's like taking mini breaks to connect with yourself. It can be a quick moment of deep breathing, noticing how you feel, or just appreciating the present. It's like giving yourself little hugs throughout the day.

Embracing Emotions

Your relationship with yourself means feeling all your emotions without judgment. It's like having a safe space inside where you can be sad, happy, anxious, or excited, and it's all okay.

Self-Care Rituals

Think of self-care as your daily dose of love for yourself. Whether it's exercise, reading, or a relaxing bath, it's about doing things that make you feel good and cared for.

Reflecting and Journaling

At the end of the day, it's like sitting down with a good friend to reflect. What went well? What did you learn? Journaling these thoughts can be a powerful way to connect with yourself.

Setting Boundaries

Having a healthy relationship with yourself also means knowing your limits and respecting them. It's like being your own guardian, ensuring you're not overstepping your comfort zone for others at your own expense.

Celebrating Small Wins

Every little achievement is a reason to celebrate. It's like giving yourself a high-five for all the small victories throughout the day.

Forgiving Yourself

You're not perfect, and that's okay. Forgiving yourself when you mess up is like giving yourself a compassionate pat on the back instead of a harsh scolding.

Gratitude

Ending your day with a sense of gratitude for yourself and your experiences. It's like saying, "Thanks, self, for being you and for getting through another day."

Developing a positive relationship with yourself is like building a friendship — it takes time, effort, and lots of understanding. But once you're there, it's one of the most rewarding relationships you'll ever have.

Creativity and Expression

Think of creativity as your playground. It's where you let your imagination run wild and free. Whether it's painting, writing, music, or even cooking, creativity is like speaking your soul's language. It's not about being perfect or creating masterpieces every time. It's about expressing yourself and enjoying the process. It's like giving yourself permission to make a beautiful mess and find joy in it.

Financial Self-Care

Let's get real about money. Alright, let's dive into the cash conversation. Financial self-care is basically cheering for your future self. It's all about being smart with your cash now so you can chill more later. And it's not just hoarding pennies or throwing cash into the stock market; it's really getting down to how you vibe with your finances. Is your money story one of those drama series, or is it more like a feel-good empowerment flick? Think of it as taking your finances out for a nice dinner to really figure out what makes them tick.

Social Connections and Community

Social wellness is all about finding your people — the ones who make you feel like you belong, the ones who get your jokes, the ones who are there for the highs and the lows. It's about building and keeping those connections that feel right. Catching up over coffee, hanging out with the fam, or lending a hand in your local community, it's all about those feels you get when you're with them. It's like every person you vibe with paints a new stroke on the canvas of your life.

Personal Development and Lifelong Learning

School's never out. Imagine life is this endless class, and you're here to soak up all the knowledge. Every sunrise is a chance to pick up something new, to add another layer to your personal growth. Whether you're diving into a new book, joining a workshop, or dabbling in a fresh hobby, it's about keeping that brain of yours hungry for more. Consider it your never-ending quest for brainy treasures.

Contribution and Giving Back

Sharing your spark. Giving back is all about letting your inner light shine on others. It's taking your own journey — the ups, the downs, and everything in between — and turning it into a beacon for someone else. Whether that means getting involved in charity, offering your wisdom as a mentor, or just being a rock for someone in need, it's about spreading that self-love to the wider world.

Physical Well-being

It's more than just sweat. When we talk about physical well-being, it's not just about the grind at the gym or keeping an eye on the scale. It's really tuning in to what your body's telling you it needs. Maybe today it's craving a peaceful yoga flow, a rejuvenating walk outside, or maybe just busting moves in your living room. It's a celebration of all the amazing things your body does for you, showing it some well-deserved love and gratitude.

Mind Health

Chillin' with your inner self. Think of your mind as your personal chill zone, a place where you need to keep the vibes good and the atmosphere serene. Mental health is all about figuring out how to keep the stress and worries at bay, whether that's chatting with a therapist, zoning out in meditation, or just enjoying some good old quiet time alone. It's like making sure your inner chill zone is a place you actually want to hang out in, keeping it calm and cozy.

Spiritual Grounding

Tuning into your soul's GPS. Whatever you believe in, having that spiritual connection is like having a GPS for your soul. It's about searching for and finding what gives your life meaning and direction, that thing that keeps you grounded and at peace amidst life's chaos. Whether that's diving deep into your religious faith, finding Zen in meditation, getting lost in the great outdoors, or just having a heart-to-heart with your inner self, it's all about aligning with your spiritual north star.

Rolling With the Punches

Imagine life's changes as waves; being adaptable means you're the surfer riding atop, making every twist and turn an exciting part of the journey. It's about seeing change not as a big scary monster but as an invitation to a dance, an opportunity to see just how flexible and creative you can be. After all, change is gonna come, whether we like it or not, so we might as well learn to tango with it and make the most out of the music life plays.

Now, diving deep into a healthy relationship with yourself, think of it as the ultimate all-in-one package deal for living your best life. It's not just about hitting the gym or meditating under a full moon (though both are pretty great); it's about the whole shebang. Loving yourself, growing a little every day, and spreading that love like confetti wherever you go. At the end of the day, the longest relationship you're ever gonna have is with yourself. So, make it a good one. Feed it good vibes, give it some love, and watch how it paints every corner of your world in vibrant colors.

WRAPPING UP THE VALENTINE'S DETOX JOURNEY

We're at the end of our Valentine's Detox journey, and what a ride it's been! It's like we've been on this cool road trip, discovering new parts of ourselves, understanding love, and learning to vibe with life in a whole new way. Let's take a moment to look back at the amazing insights and shifts we've experienced.

Finding Ourselves in the Love Labyrinth

Our journey kicked off with an eye-opener: We hold the pen that writes our love stories. Remember when we talked about the patterns in our relationships? It was all about understanding that how we allow others to treat us sets the stage for our romantic experiences. It's like giving someone the script to our lives and saying, "Here, you play the lead." But then we realized, hey, that's our role!

Hero vs. Victim: Flipping the Script

One of the coolest parts was exploring how we could be our own heroes instead of playing the victim. It's like switching from a side character in our story to the main hero. We looked at how staying in those energy-sucking relationships was actually us handing over our superpowers to someone else. Being our own hero meant stepping up, making bold choices, and writing a story that's all about self-love and respect.

The Dance of Relationships

We waltzed through the different stages of relationships, didn't we? From the dizzying heights of the love bubble to the comfy vibes of the chill love stage, each phase was like a different dance. And let's not forget about those moments of eyeing the exit or embracing the single life. It's been a journey of figuring out what makes us happy and what kind of love dance we want to be part of.

Unpacking Our Emotional Baggage

This was big, right? We dug deep into our emotional closets and started unpacking. It was all about letting go of the stuff that no longer served us — like those old beliefs and fears that kept us in toxic relationships. It felt like spring cleaning for the soul, making space for new, positive vibes to come in.

Gratitude: Our Secret Superpower

We discovered that gratitude isn't just saying "thanks." It's this super-power that changes the way we see the world. It's like putting on these awesome glasses that make everything brighter and more colorful. Gratitude helped us turn our focus from what we don't have to all the amazing things we do have. It's been a game-changer in how we vibe with life and love.

The Big Picture: Healing and Moving Forward

Finally, we tackled the big one: healing from past hurts and moving forward. It's like we've been carrying this heavy backpack, and we've started to take out the stuff that weighs us down. We've learned to be kinder to ourselves, to practice self-care, and to create a life that's about joy and fulfillment.

The Final Note: Embracing Our Journey

Let's take a moment to pat ourselves on the back. We've come a long way. We've laughed, maybe shed a few tears, but most importantly, we've grown. This journey's been all about discovering that the most epic love story we'll ever write is the one with ourselves.

So, here's to moving forward with hearts full of self-love, minds open to new possibilities, and lives ready for amazing adventures. It's not just about surviving Valentine's Day; it's about thriving every day. Remember, the best is yet to come!

Confronting the Energy Vampires

Our Valentine's Detox journey wouldn't be complete without address-ing those Energy Vampires. Remember how we talked about those people in our lives who just drain us dry? Like those sneaky characters in a horror movie, except these are real-life people who leave us feeling exhausted. We learned to spot them, understand how they operate, and most importantly, how to keep our energy safe. It's like learning to be a vampire hunter in our own lives — identifying who's sucking the joy out of our days and taking steps to protect ourselves.

Taming the Inner Vampire

And then there's that part of us that sometimes sabotages our happiness. We all have it, lurking in the shadows, feeding off our insecurities and fears. This journey taught us to shine a light on this Inner Vampire, to understand its tricks and how to tame it. It's been about transforming this Inner Vampire from a foe to an ally — using its insight to empower us rather than drag us down.

By recognizing the power of these Energy Vampires and our Inner Vampire, we've taken huge steps in protecting our emotional wellbeing and ensuring our journey towards self-love and healthy relationships isn't hijacked. It's like equipping ourselves with garlic and holy water, but for the soul.

Self-Discovery and Empowerment

So, as we close the book on this chapter of our Valentine's Detox, let's celebrate the whole journey. From understanding the dynamics of our relationships to dealing with external and internal vampires, we've covered a lot of ground. We're walking away with a toolkit full of self-love, awareness, and resilience.

Here's to a future where we're not just surviving but thriving; where our relationships are sources of joy, not drain; and where our Inner Vampire becomes a symbol of our strength and growth. We've turned the page to a new chapter, one where we're the heroes of our story, dancing to a rhythm that's uniquely ours. Cheers to that!

ONE MORE THING...

Are you the energy vampire you have been complaining about?

It's quite the catch-22. After journeying through this book, a mirror might have been held up to your own behaviors, revealing traces of those energy vampire qualities you've been learning about. So, what's the next step if you see a bit of yourself in these pages? First off, remember that walking away from a relationship should always be a last resort.

It's worth exploring every avenue to mend and heal what's broken. This could mean stepping into the world of therapy or counseling, both individually and as a couple. It's a space where understanding, healing, and growth can happen.

But it's not just about external help. The real transformation begins within you. It starts with a deep dive into your own heart and mind. If you recognize that your Inner Vampire has been casting a shadow over your relationship, now's the time to embark on a personal healing journey.

Work on your self-confidence and self-image. A healthier, more positive view of yourself can be a cornerstone in rebuilding how you interact with your partner and others around you. If you've been less than kind, begin the process of changing your approach. It's about creating a kinder, more empathetic version of yourself that contributes positively to your relationship and nurtures your love.

Remember, change is a journey, not an instant flip of a switch. Be patient, be committed, and be ready to grow.

JUST GIGGLE

There's something liberating about reaching the end of a Valentine's Detox, standing on the other side of all the emotional turmoil, and just... giggling. Yes, giggling!

Giggling isn't just laughing; it's something more profound, more intimate. It's that uncontrollable, bubbly burst of joy that seems to bubble up from the very belly of your soul, reminiscent of childlike innocence. While laughter can be loud, encompassing, and shared among groups in response to humor, giggling is personal, often shared between close friends or even enjoyed alone.

It's the kind of sound that lights up a room with its purity and simplicity. Giggling has a way of breaking down walls, connecting us to a time when joy was unfiltered and free from the complexities of adult life. It's a reminder that, at our core, there's a part of us that remains untouched by life's harsher realities—a part that finds delight in the simplest of things, much like a child discovering the world for the first time.

Giggling is the heart's way of whispering, "It's okay to let go and just be." It's about looking back at the rollercoaster of toxic relationships, the drama, the highs and lows, and finding the humor in the fact that, well, we played a starring role in our own soap operas. This chapter is an ode to the art of letting go, forgiving ourselves, and embracing the power of laughter through something I like to call Giggle Yoga.

Imagine realizing that the key to unlocking your emotional handcuffs wasn't held by anyone else but you. That's right. It was your own thoughts, beliefs, fears, doubts, judgments, and sky-high expectations that crafted the script of your past relationships. It's like discovering you've been the director of your own drama without even knowing it. And when this realization hits, what can you do but laugh?

Giggle Yoga isn't about bending yourself into a pretzel while laughing maniacally (though, if that's your jam, go for it!). It's a metaphorical practice, a way of life that involves looking at your reflections, your missteps, and your 'what was I thinking?' moments with a light heart. It's laughing at the absurdity of our human experience, at the ways we complicate love, and at the sheer comedy of realizing we've had the power to change the channel all along.

Taking 100% responsibility for our lives, with no room for blame or victimhood, is incredibly empowering. It's acknowledging that every choice, every reaction, and every belief was ours to make. And while that might seem daunting, there's a peculiar strength that comes from owning our part in our stories. It's a strength that's best celebrated with a giggle.

Why giggle, you ask? Because giggling and laughing is the antithesis of toxicity. It's impossible to hold onto anger, resentment, or sadness when you're genuinely giggling from the belly of your soul. Laughter brings us back to the present, to the simplicity of the moment, and reminds us that life, in all its complexity, is also ridiculously funny.

So, as you step forward from your detox, carry with you the lightness of laughter. Forgive yourself for the times you forgot your worth, for when you let fear guide your steps, and for any moment you thought you needed someone else to complete you. Forgive, let go, and giggle at the beautiful messiness of being human.

As you practice Giggle Yoga, remember to laugh not just at yourself but at the collective comedy of human relationships. We're all stumbling, learning, and growing in love. And when we can share a laugh over our shared follies, we find a common ground more solid and healing than any romantic gesture.

In the end, "Just Giggle" is more than just a chapter title—it's an invitation. An invitation to lighten up, to find joy in the journey, and to celebrate the incredible resilience of the human heart with laughter. So, take a deep breath, look back at your path with kindness and humor, and let your heart giggle. Because sometimes, laughter truly is the best medicine.

There arrives a moment in life
when you step back from the chaos
and those who brew it.

Choose to be around those
who bring joy and laughter.

Let go of negativity
and cherish the positive.

Embrace those who care for you,
and wish well for those who don't.

Life's too fleeting to not embrace joy.

Stumbling is inevitable in life,
but rising again is truly living.

It is your life.

Rise and shine.

—David Lloyd Strauss

GET PUBLISHED

Do You Have a Story of Survival or Transformation?

"You should write a book about your story..."

If you've ever heard these words, or if your journey feels like a page-turner just waiting to be penned, then you're in the right place.

David Strauss is here to make that happen – with flair, fun, and maybe even a dance move or two!

Author Coaching

Editing

Publishing

Done for you OR Done with you!

Go to: DavidStrauss.com

David's 1ˢᵗ Book

David's 3rd Book

SECOND MOUSE
GETS THE CHEESE

FEELING TRAPPED BY MISTAKES, BAD ADVICE OR INEXPERIENCE?

Upgrade your thinking
Make smarter decisions
Build strong relationships

DAVID LLOYD STRAUSS

WHAT *if* TODAY *were the* DAY?

a pocket book by
DAVID LLOYD STRAUSS

Egg Nog, Elves & Oy Vey!

Holiday Family Drama Survival Guide

DAVID LLOYD STRAUSS

ABOUT DAVID STRAUSS

When a falling rock collided with David's head while exploring ancient ruins, his 5-year recovery became his life's purpose.

DAVID...

An author coach, thought leader, and transformational speaker with a story of thrills, resilience, and transformation. David's life reads like an adventurous novel, filled with twists and turns that shaped him into the transformational author, coach, mentor, and Life Strategist he is today.

From Tragedy to Triumph

At just 15, David's world crumbled with the death of his mother. Facing life alone as a runaway at that young age, he summoned a relentless spirit that propelled him through high school, college at CU Boulder, and into a world of boundless exploration.

A Brush with Death, A Gift of Destiny

While exploring ancient ruins, a falling rock struck David's head. The rockfall was a defining moment that created the opportunity for David to reinvent himself, beginning with those daring moments at ground zero of his collision with the rock. This incredible journey has forged his philosophy as a thought leader.

Scaling Heights, Diving Depths

David's zeal for life extends to scaling the 23,000-foot summit of Aconcagua, Argentina, plunging into the depths with SCUBA, and taking leaps from planes and bridges through skydiving and bungee jumping. His adventurous pursuits are metaphors for his Life Coaching philosophy: Embrace life fearlessly.

Philanthropist And Community Volunteer

David's world travel and philanthropic endeavors reveal a man who seeks to elevate humanity. His community service and world outreach resonate with his commitment to personal growth and social impact.

Begin Your Journey With David's Coaching and Mentoring

David's unique approach is grounded in his own transformative experiences. He doesn't just talk about change; he embodies it.

From the rocky terrains to the soaring skies, from the personal hardships to global outreach, David's life is a testament to resilience, adventure, and love for people. His smile and energy invite you to join him on this remarkable journey.

CONNECT NOW!

DavidStrauss.com

www.ingramcontent.com/pod-product-compliance
Lightning Source LLC
Chambersburg PA
CBHW051520120626
46551CB00012B/1006